Praise for *Wisdom from Your Spirit Guides*

*"Wisdom from Your Spirit Guides is a beautiful,
grounded, and welcoming invitation to engage deeply and personally with
your allies in the subtle realms. It shows the perfect way to connect
with the love and support waiting there for you."*

— **Sonia Choquette**, New York Times best-selling author of
Your 3 Best Super Powers

*"James Van Praagh is the master at sharing insights and truths
that comfort and inspire.* Wisdom from Your Spirit Guides *is filled
with heartwarming stories, deep understandings, and fun exercises that
will convince anyone they're not alone in having to navigate
their wondrous adventure through time and space."*

— **Mike Dooley**, New York Times best-selling author of
From Deep Space with Love

"In his new book, Wisdom from Your Spirit Guides, *James Van
Praagh helps readers develop an understanding that we all have
access to something higher within and beyond ourselves. This book
shows us how to become consciously aware of our relationship to
our spirit guides so that we can feel more supported, inspired,
and fulfilled. I love everything about this beautiful book and I
recommend it those who are ready to enhance their spiritual path."*

— **Gabby Bernstein**, #1 *New York Times* best-selling author of
The Universe Has Your Back

*"Wisdom from Your Spirit Guides is the most comprehensive
book on spirit guides ever written. If you want to understand everything
there is to know about your spirit guardians and their messages for you,
go no further! In a step-by-step manner that anyone can master,
you will learn how to hear the secret messages from these
loving beings. Highly recommended!"*

— **Denise Linn**, internationally renowned teacher and
best-selling author of *Kindling the Native Spirit*

T0026102

WISDOM
FROM YOUR SPIRIT
GUIDES

ALSO BY JAMES VAN PRAAGH

Books

*The Power of Love**
*Adventures of the Soul**
*How to Heal a Grieving Heart**
Talking to Heaven
Reaching to Heaven
Healing Grief
Heaven and Earth
Meditations with James Van Praagh
Looking Beyond
Ghosts Among Us
Unfinished Business
Growing Up in Heaven

Card Decks

*Messages from the Guides Transformation Cards**
*The Power of Love Activation Cards**
*The Soul's Journey Lesson Cards**
*Talking to Heaven Mediumship Cards**

❀   ❀   ❀

*Available from Hay House
Please visit:

Hay House USA: www.hayhouse.com®;
Hay House Australia: www.hayhouse.com.au;
Hay House UK: www.hayhouse.co.uk;
Hay House India: www.hayhouse.co.in

WISDOM
FROM YOUR SPIRIT
GUIDES

A Handbook to Contact Your
Soul's Greatest Teachers

JAMES VAN PRAAGH

HAY HOUSE, INC.
Carlsbad, California • New York City
London • Sydney • New Delhi

Copyright © 2017 by James Van Praagh

Published in the United States by: Hay House, Inc.
www.hayhouse.com®

Published in Australia by: Hay House Australia Pty. Ltd.
www.hayhouse.com.au

Published in the United Kingdom by: Hay House UK, Ltd.
www.hayhouse.co.uk

Published in India by: Hay House Publishers India
www.hayhouse.co.in

Cover design: Tricia Breidenthal
Interior design: Karim J. Garcia

Library of Congress has cataloged the earlier edition as follows:

Names: Van Praagh, James, author.
Title: Wisdom from your spirit guides / James Van Praagh.
Description: 1st edition. | Carlsbad : Hay House, Inc., 2017.
Identifiers: LCCN 2017013618 | ISBN 9781401951375 (hardcover : alk. paper)
Subjects: LCSH: Guides (Spiritualism)
Classification: LCC BF1275.G85 V36 2017 | DDC 133.9—dc23 LC record available at https://lccn.loc.gov/2017013618

Tradepaper ISBN: 978-1-4019-5139-9
E-book ISBN: 978-1-4019-5138-2

12 11 10 9 8 7 6 5 4 3
1st edition, October 2017
2nd edition, July 2019

Printed in the United States of America

To Gabrielle O'Connor:
Thank you for being one of my earthly guides
and generously sharing your wisdom, friendship,
and love. My life is enriched with you being in it.

Contents

PART II: PERSONAL GUIDES

PART III: LESSONS FROM MY GUIDES

INTRODUCTION

This manual originates from the world of Spirit. The Spirit world is our true home and the one to which we will return when we graduate from the schoolroom we know as Earth. Because the journey here can be difficult at times, I have written this book with insights and guidance to assist in making the road a little less weary and perhaps lighter and easier. Like any instruction book, use *Wisdom from Your Spirit Guides* as a reference source on your journey. We would all love to know the secret to the road less traveled where so many fear to tread. It has taken me decades to learn the secrets of the invisible realms, and it is my joy to share this information with you. I wish such information was available to me in my early development as a medium.

The idea for this book began at one of my demonstrations. An audience member asked me to share "clues" from the Spirit world that could assist her in working through her problems. Actually, it was a common question, and one that I had answered many times, but until that moment, I had never felt my responses were adequate. That evening I sat in meditation and put a call into Spirit. I asked the Spirit world to assist me in giving the necessary advice for making our experiences on Earth more fulfilling and beneficial. I share the answers on the pages that follow. At times the information was overwhelming and difficult to interpret. Often Spirit would clarify a lesson for me by using the context of my own life experience. In other words, I was being shown moments of my own life that related to the message. It was Spirit's way of emphasizing its message in a way that I could easily understand.

The book is divided into four parts so that you can pick and choose what you need at the appropriate time. The first part describes *guides*—where they come from and what they do. There are many guides with us at various times of our lives and even lifetimes, and I will share my understanding of how a variety of guides work with us. In the second part, I share individual guides and their significance to our lives. In the third part, I present particular insights from my guides that deal with life situations and circumstances. These are the chapters in which Spirit reinforced its messages by using my past experience so that I could fully understand the essence of its lesson. And I share these stories with you. For those of you who use (or are interested in using) oracle cards, I have created an accompanying card deck called *Messages from the Guides Transformational Cards*. It's a deck of 44 messages from my guides including the nine most important lessons, which I cover in the chapters of Part III. The last part shows how to make contact with your own inner guides, making sure that you are not opening yourself to unwanted energies. As with every learning experience, it takes practice to connect with the higher sources. You will need to be patient with yourself as you apply the steps to connect with your guides. After all, your guides are always patient with you.

Even with the best of intentions, we will stumble and hit roadblocks on this journey. You have to be open to the thoughts that come from Spirit. Often our lower minds, or egos, get in the way, becoming cynical to our efforts to tap into Spirit. If you can persist through the rough patches in reaching into your higher mind, and release judgment and criticism of yourself and others, you will find more harmony and peace in everything you do.

By using the ideas in this book, you will develop an understanding that there is something higher within and beyond yourself that will give you the strength to evolve spiritually. You will realize that nothing happens by chance; you are here for a definite purpose—one that is far greater than any physical goal.

As the philosopher Rudolf Steiner stated in his book *The Way of Initiation*, "He who seeks for higher knowledge must create it within himself; he must himself instill it into his soul. It cannot be done by study: it can only be done through life."

Begin to live with your spiritual eyes open, and you will become aware of the invisible forces around you. The knowledge you receive from Spirit will transform and empower all aspects of your being.

PART I

THE GUIDES

CHAPTER 1

WHAT ARE GUIDES?

Welcome to the vast and expansive world of guides! Our guides occupy an infinite array of spiritual dimensions and may have never incarnated at all, or they can be family members and friends who we have known in this lifetime, and who have since made the transition to Spirit. Whoever they may be, guides have a keen interest in your development as a soul, and they work with you as personal teachers to inspire, influence, motivate, protect, and direct you throughout your lifetime.

Many of your guides have been with you in a variety of lifetimes; some show up for one lifetime, or for a portion of your life, or even perhaps just a fleeting moment. Guides are our friends, helping us to fulfill our destiny. Some are with us merely to comfort and encourage us when things are difficult and unsettling.

Everyone can connect with their guides. Soul-to-soul connections happen all the time, but most people don't recognize them as such. For instance, whenever you think of a deceased loved one, you probably assume the thought began with you. More probable is that your loved one (with the help of your guide) is sending the thought *to* you. A few weeks after my friend Pam got a new convertible car, she confided in me: "When I bought the car, I wasn't consciously thinking of my Aunt Jean, even though she had owned several when she was alive. Now I can't get into my car without thinking about her. Great memories of her that I haven't thought about in decades flood my mind every time I drive. I don't know what's better: the car, or the happiness I feel while driving and thinking of Jean. Do you think I was influenced subconsciously to buy the car?"

I am sure you can guess what my response to Pam was. But that conversation added fuel to my desire to write about guides. And it's not like the subject of guides has not always been present in my life. When asked about my process of mediumship, I always say that my guides control who comes in. And when doing Q&As, I am often asked:

- *Do we all have guides?*
- *Can you tell me who my guide is?*
- *Do you know what my guide looks like?*
- *How do I get in contact with my guides?*

And yet, after all that, I hadn't thought to write a book about guides. Until now. So in case you were wondering, my answers to the above questions are:

- Yes.
- No, that is a personal part of your own spiritual quest.
- No, that is a personal part of your own spiritual quest.

- It takes practice to raise your vibration to
  meet them. And I hope this book helps you
  with that.

Spirit Guides

I personally define *spirit guides* as a team of energetic beings that you have carefully chosen before your present incarnation. In turn, your *spirit team* has mutually agreed to guide you. These spirit guides reside in various levels and dimensions of the Spirit realms and usually communicate through thought and feeling.

It is very possible that you have been a guide to one or more of your spirit guides when *they* were in physical form and *you* were residing in the spiritual dimensions. The roles keep reversing as we keep evolving. This makes complete sense, especially if one or more of your current guides are family members who have passed into the higher levels. During demonstrations many of the loved ones who come through relate that they can help to steer a person in the right direction from the Spirit side far better than they could while residing on Earth.

I remember right after my mother died, I had a reading with my mentor, medium Brian Hurst, who brought my mother through and said that she was going to be one of my spirit guides for a while. *Why?* I asked Brian.

"Your mother feels she did not complete her job with you on Earth. Her destiny was to help you develop psychically but she was too afraid at the time. She wants to fulfill her promise and help you from Spirit."

As I developed my psychic abilities, I could feel my mother around me and knew that she played an intrinsic part in the expansion of my spiritual awareness. As I became more sensitive and began to trust my intuition, I only had to think of my mother and immediately I would feel a cool breeze across the back of my neck or I would smell her perfume in the air.

I remember one time that I got lost while driving a rental car to one of my events. This was before GPS. Suddenly a truck passed by me with my mother's name, *Regina*, covering its side. Instantly I knew it was a sign from her. I had faith that if I followed the truck, I would discover the route to my destination. And I did. From then on, I became aware of so many signs from my mother that indicated she was nearby and ready to help.

Loved ones in Spirit are only too happy to help us if they can. Like my mother, they will make their presence known in ways we will understand—through objects like pictures, jewelry, and souvenirs, or aspects of nature that they appreciated on Earth like birds, butterflies, flowers, or possibly their names on billboards, stores, and streets. You can begin to recognize signs from your spirit guides simply by becoming aware of the world around you as you go through your day.

Spirit guides work with us energetically. Because spirit guides vibrate at a higher frequency, it becomes necessary that we learn to raise our energy to get their messages. I will describe how to raise your energy in the last part of the book. When we raise our energy by going within, we have the ability to meet our guides in a conscious state.

Guides know that it can be difficult for us to recognize them in our conscious state, so they often come to us in our dreams. They may appear as historic figures, fantasy characters, or even animals. If they want to relay an important message, you will have recurring dreams until you understand what they are trying to convey. Loved ones who have passed over almost always visit us in our dreams. Keeping a dream journal is a good way to remember our dreams and the messages our guides and loved ones want to communicate.

In order to sense our guides, we must be self-aware. As the saying goes, we are spiritual beings having human experiences. If you want to connect with your guides, you must allow yourself to trust the spiritual world. Once you understand that the spiritual realms are not *up there* but all around you, there is nothing to fear. We have to train our minds to have a conscious connection with our spirit guides and loved ones. As we learn to interact with our spirit guides, we will feel more confident in ourselves and more comforted by their company. But even if we are not consciously aware of their presence, guides are always around to support and advise us. But a conscious awareness of their wisdom is ideal, and that is the emphasis of my book.

As you'll learn in this book, each one of us has several guides. It's up to you if you feel it is necessary to know all your guides by name, the nature of their assistance, and how they present themselves. It *is* helpful, though, to become aware of at least one guide, their preferred name, and how they choose to appear.

Earth Guides

We often believe that guides are *only* those who reside in the spiritual dimensions. This is far from the truth. Guides can be people who share your everyday life like friends, neighbors, relatives, and many times even strangers. *Earth guides* are not consciously aware of being a guide of yours, but I totally believe that pacts are made between souls before physical incarnations to help assist each other. Perhaps you had a chance encounter with someone who caused you to think about an aspect of yourself that you had never considered before. Perhaps someone said something in passing that assisted you in becoming the person you are today. Your life would have been very different if you had never met that person. Perhaps you had a childhood friend who changed your life forever. I was lucky enough to have such a friend.

When I was eight years old, I was on a mission through my neighborhood to sell as many magazine subscriptions as I could for my school. I was just about to cross the street to reach the last house of the day, when suddenly a red Chevy rumbled up to me and came to a complete stop.

"Hi there, young man!" The bellowing voice of the female driver startled me. As I turned to look, I could see her eagerly waving for me to come over. I stepped toward the car and saw a brunette woman about my mother's age whom I didn't recognize. She motioned me closer so I could shake her hand. "My name is Connie Leif. I just moved here. I have a son who is about the same age as you. Would you like a new friend?"

Connie had such a welcoming feeling, and I knew instantly that I liked her. Her warmth made me feel safe, and she treated me like an adult. "Yes," I said. "I would like a new friend."

"His name is Scott. We live around the corner. This car will be parked in the driveway. I look forward to seeing you soon." Connie pressed the accelerator and away she went. I could see her hand reach up and wave from side to side as she drove off. Her joy was irresistible.

Her son Scott and I quickly became constant companions. The odd thing was that I wanted to be his friend, not only because of him, but because I enjoyed being with

Connie. I always felt she genuinely cared about me and showered me with encouragement. She was like a second mother to me.

As I grew up, I would spend hours at her kitchen table discussing people, life, and the ways of the world. I could talk to her about anything. Looking back, I know now that she was definitely a guide of mine, and without her insights and support, I would never have believed in myself. She used to say, "Jamie, reach for the stars. I will always be there to catch you if you fall!"

Earth guides come into your life at the perfect time with the perfect words to say and make an invaluable impact on the rest of your life. Some people use the term *synchronicity* or *serendipity* to describe these chance encounters that can have such a profound effect on us. But I don't believe in accidents. I think people and events are placed on your path in accordance with the blueprint that you (with the assistance of your spiritual guides) created for yourself before you incarnated. The gift is to be able to recognize who and what has been placed before you for what they are: tools from which you learn.

Guides Are Close By

Whether your guides have physical bodies or whether they reside in the Spirit realms, you must realize that they all come together with one purpose: to make your journey in this physical dimension successful. And what makes for a successful life? Well, it's different for everyone, and it's your job to discover it. Everything that happens in your life—your soul lessons—is part of a divine plan for your spiritual growth.

Our soul lessons are not always simple and easy because Earth can be a very difficult place to navigate. Learning is not always meant to be easy. If it were, it would have little value. It is important to remember that we are being guided in all aspects of our lives—from major successes and celebrations to disappointments and sorrows. Try not to focus your thoughts on things that go wrong, and never take the good things for granted. Sometimes life events that we consider to be failures or tragedies may actually be great spiritual advancements.

Everything we do has a perfect rhyme and reason even if we don't understand it at the time. For instance, you oversleep one morning and are late for an appointment. You get frustrated with yourself for not setting the alarm. But instead of getting upset, you could think differently. Perhaps the lateness was spiritually orchestrated to prevent something else from occurring. This was the case several years ago when I was teaching at Omega Institute in Rhinebeck, New York.

After class, a staff member and I were meeting a mutual friend for dinner. We had to drive across a bridge over the Hudson River to get to the restaurant. Before the bridge, I reached into my pocket and realized that I had forgotten my cell phone in the classroom, so we turned back to get it. By the time we were headed toward the restaurant once again, we were running about 15 minutes late. When we finally got to the entrance to the bridge, traffic was at a standstill. All that we could see was a sea of red taillights. As we waited for traffic to move, we found out that there was a fatal car accident at the entrance to the bridge. When we inquired about the time it had happened, we were told *15 minutes earlier.*

So, were our lives spared by going back to get my cell phone? Did a guide make me forget the phone in the classroom? I don't know. However, I do know that from a spiritual point of view there are no coincidences, and I do believe in divine intervention. I wasn't meant to be on the bridge at that time, so perhaps my guide influenced my actions. I may never know for sure in this lifetime, but my intuition tells me that my guide interceded. What happened on that bridge was not part of my blueprint.

From the moment we take our first breath, our unseen support team is always nearby to assist and take care of us. Even in the most desperate of moments, we are never alone. There are many beings encouraging you to rise up and believe in yourself, or to find an aspect of yourself that you have forgotten that can strengthen your resolve.

How Long Do Our Guides Stay with Us?

People often ask me, *How often do our guides interchange their roles? Do we have the same guides from lifetime to lifetime?* Because our soul's energy is constantly changing, expanding, and experiencing, our guides are also changing and evolving. A guide stays with us depending on the soul level we are on and the lessons we are learning.

There is a universal law always in effect: *Like attracts like.* The guides you attract will be in sync with your level of understanding and the potential that you are fulfilling. Because life brings with it a variety of experiences, your guides work in harmony to make sure your *homework* gets done. Depending upon the different lessons to be learned, there will be some guides that will stay with you from lifetime to lifetime, while others (*specialist guides*) come into your space for one particular purpose or task, and then take a lesser role when the job is done.

In this Earth world, we hire people because of their ability to get a job done. The same is true for guides. Each one has a certain expertise they bring to us; it could simply be that they have learned a skill and are drawn to you because it's a skill that you need help with. Each arrangement is specifically tailored in accordance with your goals for this lifetime. For instance, let's say you have decided to play the piano. You have a huge learning curve ahead—reading music, mastering the keyboard, positioning your fingers, timing, listening, and so on. You hire a piano teacher to train you. Simultaneously, in the spiritual dimensions, you will attract a specific guide with mastery in that field to influence your potential abilities. When the task is complete, like its earthly counterpart, that specific spirit guide will step back as different challenges come onto your path.

Are Guides Assigned to Us?

When a soul decides to incarnate in a physical dimension, it begins the preparation for its sojourn well in advance. The soul receives advice and loving recommendations from divine beings known as the *etheric council* or *the elders*. This council governs, nurtures, and influences the overall plan of a soul's development upon the Earth. These highly evolved beings have completed their earthly incarnations and have taken the role of wisdom advisers to developing souls.

The first task of the etheric council is to make sure that the timing is right for a soul to tackle a new life. It takes into consideration a soul's karmic obligations, learning patterns, and that the appropriate opportunities exist on the Earth plane that a soul requires for its own particular development. During a meditation, I learned that before I incarnated several guides were assigned to me. I was told that these guides were eager to work with me because they wanted to advance their own personal growth by sharing their knowledge and helping to influence others through me.

When I speak about the council, I am talking about highly evolved souls whose wisdom and experience are used to help you create a blueprint for your incarnation into the physical. Don't think of them as judges or authority figures. They are counselors who only have your best interests at heart; what is best for you is what is best for all. The council assists you in preparing a team of guides that is best suited to help you fulfill the blueprint that you have all formulated to best serve your soul's evolution.

I welcome the assistance of my guides because they intercede, interact, and advise me about possible future outcomes and alert me to the many physical and psychological ramifications of certain situations. With them helping me, I am able to help others.

A Sacred Contract

There may be many other reasons why certain guides stay with us. I must admit that, with my human brain, I'm not capable of fully understanding all the details. But from my work with the spiritual realms, I do believe there is an agreement between all the parties concerned that with each incarnation a *sacred contract* will be put into effect. The word *sacred* here denotes *blessed* or *reverent*.

Our sacred contract is made up of destiny points for the coming life. These are incredible opportunities given at specific times of which we can take advantage. There are also many soul lessons that were not completed successfully in previous attempts, and in the coming incarnation, a blueprint is created in which that particular lesson will be likely to succeed. This is when our guides come to our aid. They help us recognize these moments and influence us to utilize our free will, faith, and belief in ourselves to use the opportunity that will help us to learn and grow.

As you operate together with your spirit guides, it is of mutual benefit, for by assisting you in this lifetime, it will further support them in their growth as well. Whether incarnate or discarnate, both goals are one: to evolve spiritually. Once a blueprint has been agreed upon, your guides help you and your soul family determine what roles you will all be playing during your upcoming incarnations. The selection of roles is determined by many factors, but the dominant reason is the fulfillment of karmic obligations while still creating an environment for the growth and evolution of the souls involved. It would be ideal if your blueprint were only focused on your soul's evolution, but karma (the law of cause and effect) plays a huge role because your words and actions in previous lifetimes influence future lifetimes. The more consciously aware you become of the wisdom from your guides, the less karma you create that will have to be addressed in a future blueprint. The cast of characters (which consist of mothers, fathers, siblings, spouses, and children) are selected, and usually from one's own soul group. Again, it's a mutually beneficial arrangement for all. But occasionally a soul is needed for your incarnation that exists outside of your soul family.

My husband, Brian, once had a psychic reading long before I met him. The psychic told him that it was rare for her to read someone who had what she called a "maverick soul." She told him that a maverick soul does not belong to one soul family, but instead acts as a "free agent" who agrees to assume a role in another's soul's incarnation because the maverick soul possesses qualities that can't be found among the existing soul family. Brian didn't understand what it meant at the time, but years later, when he told me about it, I totally believed it. I think the guides on my spirit team had special plans for me, and they needed someone to play the role of my spouse who could handle my peculiar needs of being a well-known spiritual teacher in the world. And it worked, because I'm telling you now that you wouldn't be reading this book with my name on the cover if I didn't have Brian in my life.

There is always room for change if a soul decides to modify its course of action while on Earth. Guides at the highest level will not only work with one particular individual but also with the entire soul group. Therefore, many of us in a soul group, such as a family, share the same guide or guides. Also, we share a team of guides who assist in our work environment, or at school, or in a special activity. When I was in a development circle with a group of other psychic individuals, there certainly was a team of guides working with us to enhance our extrasensory faculties.

Remember that a sacred contract sets forth a mission composed of souls and experiences in the physical and spiritual dimensions that come together so that we can live out certain moments on our journey. Not only do we learn, but others—some of whom we don't know—also learn greater awareness, understanding, and love. The connectedness we have with each other is far beyond our ability to realize with our limited earthly brains.

Spirit Guides Are Always Learning

There is a mistaken assumption that while our souls are in Spirit that we are finished learning. Nothing could be further from the truth. Guides in Spirit never stop learning. As they influence us at certain pivotal points, they learn to expand and evolve as teachers.

By the time souls reach advanced levels of spiritual awareness, their aptitudes are well known in the Spirit world. As guides, they are given occupational duties commensurate with their abilities. There are many different avenues of approach to learning. Eventually all of us will arrive at the same end in acquiring spiritual wholeness.

I believe Earth is one school of many schools comprised of places, spaces, galaxies, and dimensions. Earth is rich in opportunities with an abundant population of advanced souls, young souls, and all those in between. Our earthly environment is composed of various degrees of belief systems, archetypes, and patterns that force a soul to be tested, and eventually to advance. Although our spirit guides can be highly evolved, they are always willing to learn more. Believe it or not, in certain circumstances a spirit guide can learn more from you than you learn from them.

CHAPTER 2

WHERE GUIDES RESIDE

I once asked the Spirit world to describe Earth from their point of view, and the reply still staggers my mind. *James, your world is a mere grain of sand on the beach in relation to the enormity of the spheres, planes, universes, and worlds within worlds.* This concept is incomprehensible to us while the information is filtered through our human brains, and I want you to keep this in mind when you attempt to understand the various levels and worlds where guides reside.

When I first started developing as a medium, I had a dream one night that has stayed with me to this day. Spirit people conveyed to me the layout of their worlds in a way my human mind might be able to understand. The design clearly appeared as an inverted triangle. Think of an upside-down food pyramid. At the pointy bottom was human life and everything related to Earth as we understand it. Above this level were the unseen levels where spirits and spirit guides reside. Above that level were higher guides, and above them were prophets, ascended masters, and angelic beings. As one goes higher in the pyramid, the vast network of worlds within worlds grows exponentially. And it is important to understand when attempting to understand these levels, they are not delineated as we would think with the earth mind, but each will effortlessly blend into the other subtly.

When I speak of a vast network, I am referring to the infinite number of vibratory dimensions and realms that are invisible to humans. To the spirits inhabiting them, these realms are very real and substantive. Every being is on some level of this pyramid, depending on how well they have learned their spiritual lessons. To reach the higher levels, souls have released all earthly ambitions and desires, completed their soul lessons, and are one with the Source Energy.

Because of the complex and intricate design of the world within worlds, there are guides that are familiar with Earth and have mastered a particular branch of study, others who occupy worlds that we could not comprehend, and spirit specialists who influence us from higher, more ethereal vibrations of intelligence.

The Realms

As you take this journey, I would like you to become aware of a bit of spiritual geography so you can understand the worlds that surround you. The following is a brief breakdown of the main spiritual levels as I know them. This quick look is merely the tippy-tip of the iceberg. There are endless levels, spaces, and planes of existence. To simplify your understanding of these realms, realize I am not speaking about a place but rather a level of awareness, or a sphere of consciousness, where an aspect of your soul and a guide, attuned to that aspect, come together.

I love to make the analogy of the spiritual dimensions to that of a house with many rooms. For example, you prepare food in the kitchen but serve it in the dining room. At the end of the day, you leave the living room to go upstairs to the bedroom. Although each room is independent, you are still in the same house. All is part of the same structure under one roof. Each dimension is uniquely individual yet part of the One.

The Physical Dimension

This physical dimension, our Universe, is a place of *form*, and it is at the bottom level of the pyramid. But our Universe is certainly not the only physical dimension where we learn basic awareness. We, in our roles as humans, have chosen to focus one aspect of our soul's attention on this "Earth" experience even though our souls are experiencing existences in other physical and spiritual dimensions simultaneously. Remember, there is no such thing as linear time. It is a necessary tool for humans to function, but it's an illusion. All your "past" lives and "future" lives are happening now. "Now" is all there is. It is the only place where your power resides. You are unable to change the past, and the only time you can alter your future is now.

Even though you are an eternal soul, the human world is ruled by the ego or lower mind, and you have willingly chosen to forget your divine heritage. But why? Souls take on this dense, uncomfortable world of matter to develop their awareness by living various experiences (such as fear, loneliness, and isolation) that are not available to them in other realms. But we are never alone. We have our guides and our soul family constantly encouraging us while we work our way through this school called Earth. Our soul family doesn't always consist of humans, though.

Animals as Guides

On the physical level, guides can also come to us as animals. We are well aware of service dogs for the challenged, bomb-sniffing dogs that roam our airports to protect us, therapy dogs and cats in hospitals and nursing homes, and all the other animal support on the planet. Don't ever think of animals as subhuman; they are often highly evolved beings. People love to say that pets are great because they show us unconditional love. While that may be true, I believe the best thing about pets is that they activate unconditional love *in us*.

Wild animals are guides to those who care for them. Zookeepers; animal experts like Jane Goodall, Jack Hanna, and Jeff Corwin; and all people working to protect the animal kingdom will often express how much they learn about themselves from the animals that they care for and love. Animals not only teach us about our physical environment but also about our human potential.

From 2002 to 2003 I had a syndicated TV show called *Beyond*. It was a wonderful experience, and I was grateful for the opportunity to share my beliefs about death and the other side with a large viewing audience.

One of my favorite readings from the show involved a pet. "Someone here lost a dog—the dog had to be put down. It was a German shepherd."

David, a young man in the audience, stood up and validated the information. "She comes right up and jumps on you," I said with a smile.

Immediately, I could see several audience members get choked up. I continued, "The dog was very appreciative. She misses the car rides." The young man nodded.

"You initially got her as a watchdog, but that didn't work out." The audience laughed as David smiled and nodded his head. "I want to say that the animal appreciates all that you did for her. She was in pain. Her hind legs were not good. You had to carry her around for the last month."

I said, "I know you didn't have plans to be here today. But can I say that I feel you were *led* here?" David looked up to the ceiling trying to rein in his emotions. I continued, "The dog has been sitting on your lap the whole show. She's a smart dog, and she loves you. She wants to thank you for making the right decisions for her."

After the show, David was interviewed by the host, Lisa Canning. "David, did you think it strange that your dog showed up?"

David showed Lisa a photo of his dog that he carries with him. "Not really. I had a bond with my dog. Her hind legs gave out, and we had to put her down. It was the hardest thing I had to do. After hearing everything James said, I believe the dog did bring me here. It was a reading I will never forget."

On a more personal note, I have a story about a dog that saved me, and I know that my guides intervened and had her sent to me. It was spring 2010 and I was driving in San Diego. As I waited at a four-way stop sign, I kept watching a young girl on the sidewalk holding a wiggling puppy. When my turn at the intersection arrived, the puppy flew out of the girl's arms and dashed across the street. I had been aware of the whole thing, so

I remained at a full stop; unfortunately, the driver facing me proceeded through the intersection and ran over the dog. I had never seen anything like this before, and here I am with a front-row seat.

I jumped out of my car and went to the puppy, who was writhing in pain. The little girl and her mother arrived and picked up the puppy. I was being honked at, so I got back in my car, drove through the intersection, and pulled over. By the time I got back to the scene, a policewoman was there consoling the owners. She looked over at me and before I could ask the question, she shook her head. The puppy didn't survive.

I drove back home in shock. The scene kept playing back over and over in my head. For a week, I couldn't concentrate during the day, and I had trouble sleeping at night. One night in a dream, one of my guides came to me and told me that help was being sent to me. I was told to go to the shelter where Brian and I had rescued our dog Boo Radley a few months before. I was told that a dog would be there that would heal me.

We drove to the shelter that day and I perused the kennels looking for my healing dog. I was certain that I would know him/her on sight. I had made a complete circuit of the kennels and I didn't have a connection with any of the dogs. I sat down in the lobby and hung my head. I knew that my dream had been real. Right before we left, I glanced back down the row of kennels and I saw a white face in the last one. That kennel had been empty before. I walked over to the kennel and I saw a white Jack Russell terrier girl with one black-spotted ear and one ear that was solid black. She rolled over and showed me her freckled tummy when I approached. I knew instantly that this was my healer.

We took her home and we bonded immediately. Since Brian got to name Boo Radley, it was my turn to name our new girl. I mulled a few names over but couldn't come up with something that I liked. The next day while meditating, a spirit woman came to me and told me that she was my great-aunt and that we had never met in the physical. She told me that my dog should be called Maisey Mae. And so it came to be. She is my angel, my protector, and my healer, sent to me by my guides in my time of need.

Besides animals, in nature there are guides that are protectors of the earth's elements. They comprise the devic kingdom—fairies, devas, sylphs, gnomes, and others. These are not imaginary, fanciful, or fictional. Nature guides are real and inhabit forests, mountains, oceans, rivers, and the air we breathe. When you build your awareness and sensitivity, you can feel beings that inhabit gardens, parks, trails, and all natural settings. If these guides do not want you to enter certain areas, you will feel compelled to go in another direction. It is up to us to pay attention to the subtle intuitive messages nature guides transmit.

I often talk to nature guides in my garden, especially after a tiring tour. They help to ground all the scattered energy I have accumulated and bring me back to my center. You probably don't know this about me, but if Spirit hadn't called upon me to use my talents to lecture and write, I would have been extremely happy as a landscaper. I can be out watering and planting for hours— it's a form of meditation for me. I recently moved about an hour south of the home I had lived in for 17 years. I had turned what was a sad yard into a beautiful garden at that house, and now I have the opportunity to do it again. The nature guides are so happy and grateful when you take the time to give some love and attention to the place where they reside. Spirit people will also work in unison with the devic kingdom to bring messages to living beings through plants, flowers, butterflies, birds, and trees. So it's vitally important to keep your nature-space healthy.

Your team of guides is always at the ready to bring the higher elements of wisdom into your human awareness through your Higher Self. Your Higher Self is the greatest aspect of your soul. It is your bridge to the higher realms. When you agreed to incarnate, you did so knowing that the awareness of your true self would be refocused to the physical dimension. It needs to be focused here for you to navigate. But realize that just like the colors of a rainbow, there are many shades, tones, and degrees of color that comprise your soul essence, and that the real you exists on all spiritual levels.

The Astral Dimension

Many of us are familiar with out-of-body experiences (OBE) or near-death experiences (NDE). People with these experiences often relate how it feels when they leave their bodies and move toward a beautiful white light. These experiences have helped many to understand that death is merely a transition from one state of being to another. Our soul can never be destroyed; it is whole, perfect, and immortal. Therefore, as I have said to audiences around the world, *"There is no death."* At death, the human body is released, and the soul enters the astral dimension.

The astral world looks very similar to our physical world; it is made up of a variety of kingdoms, countries, planes, levels, and points of space inhabited by a variety of souls with various belief systems. Although the astral energy is lighter and more refined than our human world, it does have physical commonalities like houses, parks, schools, gardens, streets, monuments, and the like. It is here we realize that our bodies are merely shells for our souls. Illness and age are no longer present; we feel young and vibrant once again. In this dimension we reunite with our deceased family members, friends, pets, and guides who have served us through the recent lifetime.

Many of us don't know it, but we often travel to the astral dimension when we are dreaming. I often explain to audiences that when loved ones appear in our dreams, it is not because they have "come down" to visit; it's because we have visited them in the astral dimension. Because this dimension vibrates at a very rapid rate—at the speed of thought—one does not need to speak with words. Thoughts actually materialize and, like it or not, everyone knows what you're thinking.

The Etheric Dimension

After the soul has adapted to a new state of life and moved through the many layers of the astral realm, it will eventually have an *inner calling* to expand its knowledge and move to another level of awareness known as the etheric realm. In esoteric wisdom schools, it is believed that when a soul moves its awareness into the etheric level, it goes through a *second death*. It sheds any remaining earthly characteristics and inclinations in order to advance to this higher spiritual sphere—the first true heaven world.

Over the years people have asked me why they can no longer hear messages from their loved ones. I believe it is because their loved ones have evolved to a higher expression and moved into the etheric level.

Spirit once presented me with an image describing this realm. It was musical notes that possessed color and texture, all vibrating at different speeds. And I could sense that the notes meant something, but their meaning was beyond my comprehension. If Earth is the dimension of words, and the astral is the dimension of thought, then the etheric is the dimension of symbols. So, if our thoughts and words and deeds are made up of colors and patterns, and each day we are constantly composing and adding something new, we must be mindful of our thinking and how we express ourselves. When we arrive in the etheric realm, we will experience the full force of our earthly composition.

The Spiritual Dimension

This is what humans think of as heaven, a place of incredible beauty and creativity, where all the various layers of belief systems come together as one. It is the realm of the greatest thinkers and philosophers. Spirits in this dimension are all at an equivalent level of spiritual understanding and wisdom; they live in perfect joy and harmony as pure light and love with one another.

Colors play a significant role in the spiritual dimension. Think of the movie *The Wizard of Oz*. The first 10 minutes are shown in black and white, but when Dorothy lands in Oz and opens the door of her room, she steps into the vividly colorful land of the yellow brick road. That is the difference between the earth plane and the spiritual dimension. In the spiritual dimension, the color waves are so bright and expansive, and they burst with complexity and clarity. On Earth the variety of colors is very limited, but in the spiritual dimension, the waves of color work together, energizing, transforming, and beautifying everything to its maximum potential.

For instance, a rainbow may gently touch the valley below with one of its colors, instantly transforming the valley to the same lovely color, feeling, and harmony of that particular ray. Here a luminous light permeates all. Think of buildings without ceilings covered only by this brilliant light.

In this spiritual world, advanced souls meet to discuss higher forms of creativity, philosophy, and service. All thoughts are elevated to experience a higher appreciation of beauty. Each soul feels a unity with the One Source. There is a sense of freedom as every soul assists and complements each other.

This is a very high level of spiritual evolvement, and when souls in this dimension choose to incarnate, they bring the influence of the spiritual realm with them. These are our spiritual leaders.

The Celestial Dimension

Often referred to as the angelic realm, the celestial dimension is where souls understand that they are symbols of the great creative light and are indeed containers of divine love. Only those of the highest good and quality of character evolve to this dimension. Spirits on this level have total awareness.

The celestial dimension is the domain of the ascended masters, avatars, and archangels—those who have mastered the world of ego and have transcended material craving. The souls of humans you may be familiar with such as Saint Francis of Assisi, Lao Tzu, Mahatma Gandhi, and Nelson Mandela reside on this level. Ascended masters are those who have shown unconditional love while on Earth and no longer work as personal guides but instead influence mass numbers of souls.

Avatars such as Jesus and Buddha work with all religions to bring harmony and unity. Although they are worshipped as separate beings, I believe they are symbols of the One Source to which we all belong. It is *very important* to understand that although these figures may receive glorious adoration, they are not separate from you, but a part of you. All manifestations at the celestial level of life flow directly from the Great Spirit or One Source.

This realm is way beyond human comprehension because everything exists as waves of energy that correspond directly with the affection that each has for one another. For example, flowers are not merely seen; they are celebrated for their beauty and aroma, which enliven the atmosphere. They are surrounded with perfect musical harmony that directly corresponds to their colors. Everything blends into the divine light, and *all is one.*

Spirits at this level know the actual process for the construction of what we call *reality.* Everything is shared among the masters and guardians of this world. It is as if a divine orchestra is playing, and the colors of great minds blend together with the colors of musical notes in complete unison for the enjoyment and enlightenment of all. Creative endeavors are not the same here as those conceived in the physical world. On this level the energy of love and light is within all things.

How Guides Influence Us

Guides are invested in us and play an influential role in our daily experiences. I think our innate desire to communicate with our guides is really our desire to know and understand ourselves better. Several years ago during one of my workshops, I asked my guides to show me how they inspire us with the wisdom of the higher spiritual levels. They showed me a vision of a waterfall, but instead of water, it was beautiful colors cascading from the heavens. The colors would break apart into separate droplets and anoint our heads. I often wonder if that is where the symbolism of religious baptism originates. Nevertheless, to this day I often use colored water imagery in my daily meditations.

The light beings from the highest levels transmit wisdom to the guides in the lesser levels; those guides, in turn, add their spiritual insight and knowledge and transmit that to the next level, and so forth and so on, until the information reaches our human understanding. Imagine the upside-down pyramid—eventually the inspiration comes to the point at the bottom, like a funnel.

Usually, if someone is *channeling* information in a *trance* state, he or she is receiving the end result of pure thought that originated in the etheric realms or above. All the characteristics of the various levels of awareness are downloaded into the human channel. When the motivation of the channel is to be of service, and their ego has stepped away, then the purer the information is of the transmitted thought.

CHAPTER 3

UNDERSTANDING YOUR GUIDES

Based on the many dimensions discussed in the last chapter, I want to give you a better idea of how to work with your guides and how to understand the purpose of their existence in your personal life. While most guides have had physical experiences and may appear with physical forms and the personalities they once experienced, there are many others who don't.

The guides who don't present themselves with human characteristics have gone into the higher realms and are free of earthly trappings. Also, the wisdom that you receive as *inspiration* from the Spirit realms may be the product of several guides melding their thoughts into one. This can be confusing for those of you who want to know what pearl of wisdom is coming from what particular guide. It may be difficult for our human minds to distinguish one personality from the many. And these beings are not necessarily ones with human characteristics.

The Expression of Guides

In my workshops, I have students do an exercise to surrender their egos and allow a guide of theirs to come through, either visually or through writing. The process occurs when the guide enters a person's auric atmosphere and blends with the soul aspects of the Higher Self. In these workshop settings, the guides do their best to present themselves as something we can understand.

One student, Sandra, said, "I became aware of several guides surrounding me. When I asked their names, I realized right away that they didn't have any—that they were at a very high vibration and that names were not necessary. Two of them appeared to me as men dressed in light-colored robes that seemed to be made of a glistening, almost glowing material. Under the robes was just pure light. I knew that they appeared to me in robes so I could understand that they were beings."

Another student named Toni shared her experience. "I picked up on a guide and instead of showing me a physical appearance, I *felt* the reason why we were working together. He telepathically told me that he was working with my ego-identity as Toni, that he wanted me to lighten up on myself. I asked questions telepathically, and he seemed to know what I was going to ask before I got the thought out, and he answered with complete compassion and kindness. He made me feel that any guilt and judgments I was feeling about myself were temporary and not real, and that I had to learn to appreciate who I really was, not what other people thought of me. I knew that he was in my life so that I would appreciate my talents and abilities."

Another student identified her guide as an Egyptian scribe who presented with a scroll of papyrus and stained fingers. She felt compelled to write the message down, which seemed apropos considering her guide's earthly vocation. She read the scribe's message to the other students.

"My dear one: Rise up into your power of being. The souls on Earth must understand their responsibility to cleanse and purify that which you call the mind. You are brave; for you freely take on the dense energetic thoughts of negativity which is not in alignment with your true nature. The laws of the Universe are perfect but you exist in imperfection. The elements that you allow into your mind, whether they are of an unwell nature or of a healing vibration, they will come to pass."

Through the years, I realize that the channeled wisdom of a guide is perfectly matched to the level of the channel's awareness. It's like TV commercials that are actually trying to sell you a TV by showing you how clear the picture is. The picture is only going to be as clear as the TV you're watching it on. I certainly have admiration for some channellers working today, but for the most part, I believe that channeled wisdom from Spirit is meant for you and not the masses.

The Energy of Guides

If you have a true desire to contact your guides, begin a regular practice of meditation. Meditation raises your energy; the more you do it, the more your energy amplifies. Meditating every day will give you the necessary discipline to let the Spirit world know that you are serious about your spiritual development. You should never feel pressured to meditate; it should feel like a vacation from daily demands instead of an obligation. As a clairsentient and clairvoyant, my communication with Spirit is through feelings and thought. Other people are more visual or cerebral.

Your guide knows the best energetic method to communicate with you. Don't be confused or frustrated if someone you know receives information from their guide visually, but you receive yours emotionally. Not everyone is going to connect the same way. Sensitive/right-brained people must protect their energies from unwanted negativity, while critical/left-brained people need to be aware of overanalyzing. As you go through the book, I will give you tips to become more discerning of the energy around you.

Questions About Guides

I want to share some of the questions that students have asked me over the years. Of course these are my personal opinions based on my life experiences and my work with the unseen world. Another spiritual communicator may have different responses. It is truly up to you to take what resonates as truth for your own soul, for no one can tell you who you are but yourself.

1. *Can I reach those beings on the highest of realms?*
   You will draw into your atmosphere
   those essences that can teach you at the soul
   awareness level your soul is currently at.
   There is no reason to teach you calculus if
   you still don't understand basic arithmetic.

2. *Do I have a specific number of guides?*
   Due to the constant shifting and
   expansion of spirit evolvement, there is never
   a finite number of guides per soul. Although
   guides may be involved with other souls
   along with you, there is a certain group of
   guides specifically designated to help with

your soul's lessons. As mentioned previously, while some are permanent, others may be temporary. Guides will grow and change dependent upon the tasks and lessons the earthly soul is experiencing.

3. *Are my guides always with me?*

Guides are in constant communication with your Higher Self. The very nature of this physical dimension is to make you think that you are separate or isolated. But that's an illusion necessary for your soul's evolution. Your guides are omnipresent, and this book will hopefully encourage you to have a conscious relationship with them.

4. *How can I learn the names of my guides?*

Names aren't necessarily significant to guides. Although some guides have incarnated many times as physical beings on Earth, they may or may not choose to present as one of those personalities. For many, names are limiting because they merely define a small fraction of their totality. You can assign a name to them if you wish, but guides would rather be recognized by an energetic feeling than by a name.

5. *How can I tell if my guides are communicating to me?*

When communication with a guide is occurring, quite often there is a feeling or sense of joy and excitement, and a piece of wisdom or an insight that will pop into your mind. You may feel a cool breeze or a temperature change. You may get a sense of expectation, like butterflies in the stomach or goosebumps. A guide may tap you on the shoulder or touch the top of the head. You may even hear your guide calling your name.

6. *Can my guides take on otherworldly characteristics?*

Yes. A guide may project an appearance that is within your reference point, such as a person dressed in period clothes with earthly features. Or it may appear as a nonphysical being, such as an angel, animal, an extraterrestrial, or various forms of light or energy fields. Our guides are multidimensional beings of light, but often they will take on human characteristics so that we can conceptualize them and know they are with us. Our human minds need to feel connected to them. When I was a developing medium, I would frequently be aware of a guide during meditation who was extremely loving and a brilliantly wise philosophical teacher. Yet clairvoyantly to me, it took on a sort of *jellyfish* appearance.

7. *Why do most guides seem exotic?*

It's the funny nature of humans that we need to conceptualize our guide as a Native American medicine man or a Chinese monk or some form of holy being. Honestly, this is what people think a guide is supposed to look like. In reality, guides can be anything from a frequency of light, to a doctor, a family member, a family pet, or a farmer. Even though some guides certainly are exotic (even awe-inspiring sometimes), each and every one is more humble and "normal" than you might wish them to be.

8.   *Are our guides all-knowing?*
    No. Even though they come from different levels of spiritual evolvement, they do not have all the answers. They are merely here to help you help yourself. Each of us has free will, and by understanding and using it, we become aware of all our possibilities. These loving spirits assist us in remembering our true power of being and potential.

9.   *Can guides be dishonest and hurt us?*
    It would not serve anyone for our teachers to be dishonest and guide us down a wrong path. That is not the meaning of a spiritual guide. When I hear this type of question, I usually point out to the person who thinks that this is possible that he or she needs to understand that those we draw close to us should always be loving beings.
    Belief in evil and/or demonic possession is a concept created by humans who feel the need to blame something that they label as "bad." Everyone has free will and is free to think and act as they will. Some people are ideologically closed off and unable to receive advice from their guides. Guides protect our free will and they must abide by those rules.

How Guides Contact Us

Some people think that guides are always whispering ideas and implanting visions into our heads. In truth, their influence is only as great as we allow it to be. If someone walks through life with blinders on, there is not a whole lot that guides can do. For others, their influence can be chalked up to good or bad luck. For those of us actively wanting to receive advice, their influence can become startlingly obvious. Besides influencing our thoughts and actions, guides create certain opportunities and manifest experiences in our lives. Think of all the different factors that must be orchestrated in order for something to seem *random*. It is mind-boggling.

Generally speaking, guides come to you by any means possible, whether subtly or through signs, in order to make suggestions and assist you in exploring a new subject or situation. Again, as I just pointed out, the more open we are to relinquishing control of thoughts, the more inviting the space becomes for them to create a successful impression. The following are the most common methods a guide will use to communicate with you.

1. *Sensing*

    Because we are souls, each of us is *clairsentient* or clear-sensing. It is the *feeling* you experience in your solar plexus when you meet a certain person or go into a certain place—there is a resonance, an aversion, or something in between. All of us first experience things in our lives psychically through our souls. *Sensing* is your soul's awareness or sixth sense. When a guide comes close, you may experience a sort of tingling or have a sense of an insight or idea beginning to form. It can be the proverbial lightbulb going on inside them.

2. *Telepathic Thought*

Many refer to this phenomenon with different labels, such as mental telepathy or clairaudience. A guide projects a thought from its mind to yours, and there is a sudden awareness of an idea, thought pattern, or information. You may receive a word, a sentence, or even a fleeting concept. Along with the thought can come a bit of a guide's personality as well. The most important aspect of this type of communication is for the person to be still to allow whatever thoughts and impressions to enter.

3. *Inspirational Thought*

This is actually a type of thought form that a guide transmits to your conscious mind. When you feel inspired about something, many times you are receiving ideas from the otherworld. Every single soul receives inspirational thoughts, but many creative people such as artists, musicians, and authors consistently say that music, lyrics, or prose is channeled through them from an "outside source."

4. *Symbols*

Depending on how a brain is genetically hardwired, guides may use symbols to get their message across. The recipient would have to set up what I call a *reference library* to define for themselves what each symbol represents. Guides send ideas into the mind of the recipient through the symbol and the person will understand the personal meaning of that particular symbol. Many mediums work symbolically or use a combination of symbols and telepathy.

5. *Meditation or Mind Journey*
Guides may also appear to you when the mind is more restful and receptive, as it would be in a theta frequency. An inviting space is created by your thought to allow guides to impart profound insights and a feeling of connection to the Spirit world. I have created several meditations in later chapters just for this purpose.

6. *Trance State*
Many guides will influence a medium in a deeper way. When a person's brain waves change from a theta state to a delta level, he or she can go into a light trance. The person is not technically asleep, but in a sleep-like state. Guides can easily merge with the recipient and carry on a conversation. This is also referred to as channeling.

7. *Automatic Writing*
This is one of the more familiar ways to reach your guides. I suggest to my students to send out a thought to their guides with a time and place to do this exercise. At the appointed time, begin by meditating and getting into a receptive space. Sit at a table in an upright position with pen or pencil and paper. Some of my students use colored pencils. Hold

the pen lightly and do not think of what to write. When you feel the energy shift, begin writing. I can't reiterate enough that you should not think of what to write. When you sense the energy shift once more, it is a signal that your guide has moved on, and the writing exercise is over.

8. *Dreams*

The most common method of contact with your guides is through dreams. A lot of people don't remember nighttime dreams— or if they do, it's sporadic. Like anything else, it takes practice and discipline. The best way to remember your dreams is to make the conscious intention before you fall asleep. Be sure to keep your smartphone, mini-recorder, or a journal by your bedside. If you wake up in the middle of the night because of the dream, a bathroom break, or a snoring partner, scan your memory for a recent dream. Record or jot down anything you remember, even if it is only an event, a thought, or a person. In time, you will get into the habit of remembering more of your dreams. At that point, you can ask a question of your guides before going to sleep. The answer may not come the next morning, but if you ask on a regular basis, your guide will send you a message.

In the next few chapters I will cover individual types of guides and their significance to us.

PART II

PERSONAL
GUIDES

CHAPTER 4

MASTER GUIDE

Like us, guides are always learning and evolving. As they help us here on Earth, we help them to sharpen their skills as guides. When we incarnate into the physical, a *master guide* is always with us. Our master guide has been involved in many of our incarnations and is usually a member of our soul family. Chances are, you have been a master guide in Spirit to one of your soul group members who is experiencing the physical.

To use a metaphor, master guides are the first in the chain of command of your spirit helpers. Information from higher realms and other guides is filtered to your Higher Self from your master guide. Many relaxed and open people have a good, although subconscious, connection to their master guide. It is the person who makes the effort to have a conscious relationship with their master guide who reaps the most rewards.

Master Guide and Guardian Angel

It's easy to confuse a *master guide* with a *guardian angel,* but the two have different roles in your life. A guardian angel doesn't really participate with your day-to-day experiences. It watches over you and will pull or push you out of harm's way when necessary. It knows when your Earth life is finished and is present at the time of your death to usher you to the spiritual dimensions.

Some of us are lucky to have a living guardian angel. This can be a soulmate who has been with you many lifetimes in many forms and has agreed to be with you this time to watch over you—your Earth angel, so to speak. I often thought of my mother as my living guardian angel. She knew that I could see spirits when I was very young. She was very protective of me and told me often that the spirits I saw were *angels.* She was a devout Catholic, and I think she wanted me to be a priest so that I would be sheltered yet able to use my psychic awareness to help those in need. Needless to say, my mother and I were best of friends and soulmates. I look forward to being with her again in Spirit.

Unlike a guardian angel whose function is to protect, a master guide's main role is to teach. The master guide inspires us to fulfill our destiny. Like a muse, a master guide motivates us to use our creativity. Sometimes a guide will communicate to us in a flash of insight. If we are in the science field, one might think of it as a brainstorm. Doctors often get help from their master guides through intuition. Creative types like writers, artists, and musicians get inspired ideas through visions and whispers.

We tend to repeat the same kind of occupation from one life to the next—your calling, if you will. You want to perfect certain attributes that your calling requires and your master guide assists you in developing the necessary attributes needed, such as patience, generosity, tolerance, dependability, commitment, or loyalty.

A master guide will always attempt to steer you in the direction that you planned in your blueprint. For instance, after I graduated from college, I wanted to be a TV comedy writer. One of my first jobs in Los Angeles was with Norman Lear's public advocacy group, followed by a stint at the William Morris Agency. Although they were peripheral jobs, I felt I was headed toward my goal of working in television. Then one day I was invited by a co-worker to a séance at the home of Brian Hurst. From that moment on, my life took a 180-degree turn.

But my dream of working in TV did eventually become a reality, just not in the way I had supposed. As a well-known medium, I was able to be the creative force behind the TV series *Ghost Whisperer*. My first book, *Talking to Heaven*, was made into a TV mini-series starring Ted Danson. I even had my own television show called *Beyond* in which I did readings for audience members and celebrity guests. So perhaps my dream of being in TV and my spiritual calling merged into one purpose, thanks to my master guide.

Golden Feather

My first encounter with my master guide was during a séance. Several spirits came through and revealed that they would be working directly with me in order to accomplish *our goals* in this lifetime.

Our goals? I thought, *who is the "we" in "our"?*

Eventually I understood the concept of my spirit team and that we were going to work together to help change the consciousness of the world, especially about death. They made it clear that to do so, everyone was obligated to bring the vibrational energy of Earth to a higher level of love by reminding people that they are responsible for their thoughts and words and deeds. As I continued with my spiritual practice, the spirits on my team were ever-changing: There were several doctors, scientists, monastic beings, and other forms too difficult to describe in words.

My master guide and I have shared many lifetimes. I remember the first time he filled my mind with his thoughts and teachings. The name he wanted to be known as was Golden Feather. Over the years, many other psychic artists have clairvoyantly attracted Golden Feather as a guide. Although his physical features share a commonality with Plains Indians, every medium who picks up on his energy is overwhelmed by the strong nature of his righteousness and respect for all humankind.

When I asked Golden Feather about his work with me, he commented that it was his duty and responsibility to bring forth a spiritual expansion and philosophy that would open the minds of the masses. His desire was that mankind would learn to appreciate a diverse world and make an effort to connect to (and feel empathy for) all living things. I was one of several channels in his *tribe* that he would oversee to bring forth understanding from the lofty spiritual dimensions. The words you are reading right now have the essence of Golden Feather's wisdom.

Although I know there are other guides who work with me, Golden Feather seems to be steering the ship. He once commented that part of the task of a master guide is to assist other guides on the team when to influence the *instrument* (that's how he refers to me) and direct them into my atmosphere when he feels it is necessary. He once described his connection with the other guides as the conductor of a ceremonial dance—think of the guides dancing around in a circle while Golden Feather is in the middle demonstrating the correct moves to make.

Whenever Golden Feather begins a channeling ritual with me, he always starts and ends with the same vital philosophy—that we all are *one energy*. As he proclaims: *To see another person as being different than yourself is to not see yourself as whole.*

He once used his Indian headdress as an analogy. *Each one is an individual feather magnificent in its own right. But when all are joined together, the strength, beauty, and the art that makes a beautiful headdress is one.*

Know Your Master Guide

You may already have an idea of your master guide by the kind of symbols you are drawn to. The best way to meet your master guide is to sit quietly in meditation. I will discuss how to contact your guides in the latter part of this book.

Think of your master guide as a teacher. What do you want to know? What areas of your life need help? For instance, if you are a parent and want to get better parenting skills, or you are starting a new job and want to do well, put out your intention to your master guide. Be specific when you do. *Dear guide, should I let my daughter go to the dance with this boy? Dear guide, what is the best way for me to get across my ideas at work?*

The key to sensing your guide's response is by quieting your mind and listening. The kind of listening I suggest is inner listening—not with your ears but with your mind. Your guide is aware of your world, and by taking the time to quiet yourself, you can enter your guide's world and vice versa.

Be mindful of the subtle shifts in energy when you are thinking of a problem or working on a solution. You are in the invisible worlds where answers and actions become very clear to you. Your master guide is giving you clues and signs and is waiting for you to connect. It's your job to become aware and learn your soul's plan for this physical incarnation.

CHAPTER 5

THE GATEKEEPER

While the master guide is said to be the "orchestrator" of your spirit team, the *gatekeeper* is your "security guard." As the name suggests, the gatekeeper is responsible for guarding the portal between the spiritual and physical worlds. In my line of work, the gatekeeper regulates the energy utilized by the spirit communicator (the deceased loved one) and the medium. It is the gatekeeper who will many times assist the new spirit in the mechanism of communicating correctly to a medium.

As I begin my readings in front of an audience or with a client, the gatekeeper assists me by lining up the communicators from Spirit who want to speak to me. Think of it like a party. There are a lot of people showing up, and there is one particular guest everyone wants to meet—the medium. They all crowd around this guest speaking at once and asking questions. The voices are too many, and the special guest cannot hear anything over the buzz of excitement.

This is what it feels like when I do Spirit communication. The gatekeeper keeps everyone who wants to speak organized and makes sure that each spirit understands the complexities of sending a thought or feeling into my mind. He tells them where to position themselves and how to project their thought impressions upon me.

For most people, gatekeepers are *protector guides* who safeguard their energy. They will give you a signal when you step into a place where the energy is negative or if you are around someone who may cause harm. You will get a clear, albeit subtle, message—whether a thought or feeling—to move away from the situation. It is up to you to act on it.

The Zulu Warrior

Over the years as I pierced the veil between worlds, it has been very interesting to watch the various gatekeepers evolve and change in both message and personality. When I first began to sit in a development circle, the second guide to approach me was this very large, black-skinned man. The loud thud of a huge spear crashing in front of me was not a good first impression. In fact, I was a bit frightened of this spirit because he did not seem *spiritual* at all. Instead, he looked like some kind of menacing warrior. My first thought was that this guy must be a lost soul that hasn't gone into the higher dimensions.

But the spirit warrior shouted in my mind that he was from the Zulu people and that he would be my gatekeeper. *My job is to protect you.* I found that so interesting because I knew literally nothing about the Zulu nation. I had to do some research about these people and their traditions.

The Zulu, or "the people of the heavens," were once made up of clans and chieftainships melded into the Zulu Kingdom by a leader named Shaka in the early 19th century. Their traditions are held by the proud people of KwaZulu-Natal, a province of South Africa. The Zulu beliefs center on honoring their ancestral spirits. The Zulu Kingdom is held in high regard by most of the people in South Africa.

When my Zulu gatekeeper introduced himself, his energy felt extremely intimidating to me. Eventually I realized that his energy is exactly what is needed to be an excellent gatekeeper. In the work that I do, it is particularly important to have a protector because when I open my energy field to the Spirit world, sometimes negative entities will try to enter. Occasionally when I am doing a reading I can sense a negative energy from a lower dimension around me, but because of my gatekeeper, this energy will not be able to cross into my electromagnetic energy field.

The Winchester House

I've often said that wherever you are, the Spirit world is always just an arm's length away, even though you are not aware of it. However, there are some places where the supernatural energy is so powerful that ghostly sightings and strange occurrences are commonplace and unmistakable. If you ever feel psychically uncomfortable in a situation, it's always good to close your eyes and call on your gatekeeper for protection.

Unevolved entities inhabit the lower astral dimension between our earthly world and the higher realms. The energy in this lower world vibrates very close to Earth's frequency. Spirits claim that it is a murky and misty dimension in appearance. In this lower world, spirits can seem like fragmented thought forms of hate, prejudice, anger, and spiritual ignorance. These spirits are stuck in a judgmental mind-set, choosing not to move into a higher, more expansive world of light. They are attracted to our earthly energy and feed off the collective negativity of our world.

Spirits from the lower astral are connected to places by their beliefs. They might have strong memories, good or bad, associated with a place, or have unfinished and unresolved business with a person. They also might be attracted to the vibrations coming from a certain area.

Recently I hosted a group of about 30 people to see one of the most famous haunted houses in America—the Winchester Mystery House. You may or may not be familiar with the story of Sarah Winchester, heir to the Winchester rifle fortune.

According to local lore, after the deaths of her husband and daughter, Sarah was told by a Boston psychic that her family was cursed by the spirits of those killed by her husband's guns, with an implication that Sarah would be the next victim. The only way to ensure her safety, the psychic told her, was to appease the spirits by building a great house for them, and as long as construction continued, her life was not in danger. Sarah moved from her home in Connecticut to a small town in California, now known as San Jose, and began building a mansion with her inheritance. Sarah kept a continuous crew of workers busy by adding rooms and hallways to her mansion over a period of 38 years. There are stairs leading nowhere and doors that open onto brick walls. At the time of her death in 1922, Sarah's house covered six acres, had 47 stairways, six kitchens, 2,000 doors, 10,000 windows, and 160 rooms!

Although the lady of the house appears to have crossed over successfully, to this day there are frequent unexplained sights, sounds, and energetic shifts reported by the staff and visitors. Odd voices, mirrors reflecting images of people from a time long ago, and specters of workmen and household servants appearing and disappearing have all been reported.

As we followed our tour guide, Janet, up a winding staircase, I started to feel the presence of Spirit. Not knowing who I would encounter, I called on my gatekeeper to protect me. I immediately felt his powerful energy like a force field. We all walked single file into Sarah Winchester's bedroom, and standing right next to Janet was a spirit woman who proudly declared this to be *her room*. I found myself drawn into telepathic communication with Sarah Winchester! Obviously her spirit meant no harm or my gatekeeper would not have allowed her energy to mingle with my own.

Sarah was friendly and let me know emotionally that she is very fond of Janet and how appreciative she is that Janet honors the house so much. Sarah wanted me to tell Janet that she also visits Janet in her dreams and tries to impress her mind with insights and trivia about the house. Janet confirmed that she dreams of Sarah (whom she obviously never met) and that factual accuracy about the house is always paramount when she gives a tour.

I think the people on the tour were hoping for a scarier encounter with Sarah, but here she was beaming with pride about her house and praising her favorite tour guide. Usually Spirit is loving and welcoming, but sometimes not so much.

Uninvited Guests

If unruly guests crashed your party, you would ask them to leave. The same goes for opening your energy field to souls who just want to "hang out" with you, perhaps due to addictions or behaviors. Unbeknownst to many people, the spirits of addicts who have not shed the lower-level energies of their earthly desires can affect the living. They can influence you and sometimes have a strong desire to reexperience their addictions vicariously through you. For example, a friend of mine named Barbara told me of her experience with *negative spirits.*

Barbara had just moved into a small house on the Venice Canals in Los Angeles. Soon after, she began to feel depressed and moody. A neighbor told her that the house was once inhabited by dope dealers and drug users. "I would have an overwhelming desire to buy cigarettes, and I wasn't even a smoker. I remember stopping at a gas station one day to buy a pack of cigarettes. That was when I knew something was very wrong."

Barbara decided to meditate and ask her guides about the house. Immediately she became aware of ghosts huddled in one of the rooms. She realized that they were former inhabitants—young drug users. "I think they are in some kind of an 'in-between state.' I don't think they even knew that they were dead," she told me.

Barbara asked me if I would help to assist these spirits to the higher levels of the Spirit world. We began by asking our gatekeepers for their assistance in bringing these beings some help. We all started to meditate and send through thoughts of love and peace. After some time, these addicts became aware of their predicament and agreed to move on to another world, where they could be freed from their earthly behaviors. After that, Barbara no longer had any desire to buy cigarettes, and her mood changed for the better.

Guarding Yourself

As you open yourself up to the Spirit world, you must learn discernment. You must be aware of the kind of thought energy you are creating and sending out into the atmosphere surrounding you. If you ask your guides for assistance, be mindful of their energy. Guides from the higher realms radiate love, peace, and joy. Beings from the lower levels are attracted to fear, anger, and all the qualities that appeal to our egos. People who are always depressed, unhappy, cynical, and/or egotistical will attract energies that reinforce similar behavior.

Because we are electromagnetic energy fields, we must realize that any abusive behaviors, such as with drugs, alcohol, food, sex, and so forth, weaken our protection and invite negative energies—whether from the Spirit world or from the earth world—into our atmosphere. Lack of sleep and poor eating habits can also lower our resistance.

If you are making changes in your life, become aware of your thoughts. Don't dwell on the past and what might have been. Be careful about joining websites to hook up with people. Be aware of the people you socialize with and where you hang out. Low-level spirits love to hang out in bars because alcohol depletes our energy fields, and we can become susceptible to not only spirits but humans with devious intentions. Just be cautious and mindful.

Protector guides can help us, but they cannot do it alone. We must be mindful of our thoughts and behavior so as not to create a world with more animosity, fear, and intolerance. As we think and behave, we create. If we are compassionate, kind, and loving, we will spread the same kind of energy to others.

CHAPTER 6

RELATIONSHIP GUIDES

One of the most common lessons that souls come to Earth to learn about is the energy of love. There are many different aspects to love—love of self, family, children, friends, co-workers, animals, community, and so forth. Of course, let's not forget love of partner, with whom we express the deepest parts of our being, such as vulnerability and sensitivity. No matter the relationship, we share a commonality with each one.

Relationships hold our most difficult lessons because we tend to have unrealistic expectations or the need to be in control—which we can never be—or we want a person to be something he or she is not. Difficulties in relationships are but lessons that we have failed to learn, so they are presented to us once again. You always have free will. If you react to something without stopping to process it first, you may create some unpleasant circumstances.

Your *relationship guide* can be quite helpful as you deal with every difficulty and distress on your journey through the lessons of love. Your spiritual development always comes first to your guides, and your relationship guide plays an important part in bringing the right people to you at the right time so that you can learn to open your heart, appreciate yourself and others, and feel worthy of love.

Love Bonds

Relationship guides are often family members and friends who have passed into the spiritual realms. The love that was created between you and your loved ones never dies because you have promised to help one another in many incarnations. In most cases a relationship guide has been with you for a multitude of lifetimes and has had a direct impact on your ability to create and sustain relations in all areas of your soul's history. During the *in-between state*, before this lifetime, your relationship guide assists you in planning your upcoming incarnation and all the relationship lessons you have decided to learn.

Relationship guides work with our unique energy to attract persons with whom we are karmically connected. Because we are part of a *soul group*, we have many *soul mates*. When you meet a soul mate, you may have a *feeling* of familiarity, good or bad. Soul mates always bring with them important soul lessons.

As I have stated many times, every soul has what I call *destiny points*. Think of destiny points as core lessons that your soul must learn in order to graduate to the next level. You always have free will, so it is up to you how and when you decide to tackle a particular lesson that has been placed on your path. The job of your relationship guide is to present certain circumstances and events as a lesson. Your guide will influence you to behave appropriately so that hopefully you will pass your test.

For example, you may have a short fuse and are quick to judge. Your guide will present someone who pushes your buttons so you can learn patience and restraint. This situation may happen quite a few times until you begin to realize that the anger you are feeling has nothing to do with the other person but rather with your own insecurities.

Perhaps you have to learn to trust. Your relationship guide will bring about scenarios in which other people test your ability to trust. Your guide doesn't leave you to fend for yourself, although often it may seem that way. Your guide will always show you a way to resolve a difficult situation. Your part is to pay attention to your thoughts and feelings so that you can remove the obstacles to your happiness and joy.

Family Dynamics

Because most of the work I do is communication with family members, I am often asked about how relationship guides help to deal with family dynamics, especially if they are dysfunctional. Again, you must realize that your relationship guide has set up lessons with you and the other members of your family by picking the roles each plays in this lifetime and the drama it entails. However, you are not enslaved by this arrangement. The purpose for our family dynamics is to rise above our circumstances and become self-realized.

There's an old saying that goes like this: *You can pick your friends, but you can't pick your family!* But you *do* pick your family; you just have no memory of doing so. Soul wisdom is always available because through many incarnations, you have played the roles of mother, father, son, daughter, husband, wife, boss, employee, friend, enemy, etc. Because you have occupied these various roles, you carry within you an awareness of each one.

Family relationships can either encourage or deter your ability to advance spiritually. Your ego will try to make one of you the victim and the other the victimizer and coax you to resolve problems with negativity or destruction. When our egos take over our higher sense of being, the results include hurt feelings, confusion, and unhappiness. But instead of repeating the same choices, we have the opportunity to make better ones and thus escape the pain that our previous choices have brought us.

Your relationship guide will try to make sure that you work through your karmic obligations by utilizing love and understanding. Sometimes your guide may impress upon you that the best solution to a broken family situation is to focus on your soul's innate wisdom. By empowering yourself, you may be able to pass that energy on to other family members and in turn, they can open up to their own spiritual truth. Using love in every relationship situation is the best tool, and the only way to progress in your spiritual evolution.

Endings

Because relationships reach beyond the romantic, our relationship guide is a major influence on the full range of relationships beyond families, from ones in business to those among neighbors, friends, and strangers. Relationships are constantly changing, and when they end, we can feel empty. There is always a reason, and we must learn to detach from expectations, fantasies, and fixed opinions.

As we alter our own sense of self-love, the energy or frequency surrounding us changes as well. You generally magnetize to you those people who are on the same vibrational frequency, and at the same time release those who are not. This is true of every soul who walks this Earth. So if a relationship ends, it means that there has been an energy shift. As one relationship ends, another will be brought to you.

Most relationship endings can be very difficult for a number of reasons—our emotional connection, unfulfilled dreams, or even misinterpretation. I am constantly reminded that souls come into our lives for the necessary time it takes for us to either teach or learn. This may take one month, five years, a lifetime, or several lifetimes, depending on the lessons.

I have shared incredible moments in my own life with some amazing spiritual teachers and associates, only to find as the years passed we have moved on to experience new relationships. If ever I am sad about losing a friendship, I think about all the wonderful times we shared while we were in school together, and I am forever grateful for having had the experience.

A Guide's Function

The overall reason we reincarnate into the human body is to have a diverse and well-rounded experience with relationships. Most people with whom you interact have had a pivotal part in one of your past lives. I often think that we are merely pieces on a chessboard and our relationship guide is involved in moving the pieces of our earthly connections in order for us to win the game. We are here to resolve any and all negative karma, not to create more.

Relationship guides want to assist you in bringing only those souls who share a mutual respect, joy, and harmony. Nevertheless, if we are completely set on being with someone even though it is not good for us, our free will may draw a person to us out of desperation. The quality and sustainability may not be there, but the desire to be with somebody can outweigh our soul's higher calling.

This reminds me of a reading I had when I was just starting my mediumship. A woman around 40 years old came to see me for a private session in my home in Hollywood. She was well-dressed and well-mannered, but also very anxious. As is my usual custom, I closed my eyes, said a prayer, asked for my guides' assistance, and began the reading.

"There is a man standing to your right. He is thin, has a pinky ring, and is smoking a cigarette." The woman's eyes lit up. "Oh my God, that must be my father." I got the impression that this man was a very heavy smoker. I could feel a lot of pressure on my chest. "Did you father have lung cancer?" She nodded. "He is showing me his lungs all black and crinkled." She began to tear up.

"He is saying he is sorry for any pain he caused you when you were young." The woman shook her head and said, "He was very strict and didn't want me to go out with boys." I continued: "He thought he was doing what was best for you." The woman quickly chimed in. "He *was* doing the best for me; I just didn't listen."

The reading went on for the next 30 minutes as an uncle and aunt came through to give the woman messages about family members. At the end, I could see this woman's expression lighten and her anxiety disappear.

"I want to explain about my father," the woman said. "I was so in love with this boy when I was 20. My father didn't trust him and didn't want me to marry him. Anything my father said, I did the opposite. I got pregnant and we got married and moved out of state right after I had a baby. My husband—who I was so in love with—was home late almost every night. I was miserable being alone most of the time with my baby. He told me he was working overtime to get extra cash. I was so in love I never thought otherwise. Then one night, the week before Christmas, he came home late again and told me that he wanted a divorce. I was shocked."

"What was his reason?" I asked.

"He told me he didn't love me and that he wasn't working late but seeing another woman. I was so devastated I wanted to kill myself. My father came to stay with me and helped me through the divorce. I should have listened to him in the first place because he was right about not trusting my husband. I couldn't see it because I was too young to understand and too in love with being in love. The funny thing about my dad was that he never said 'I told you so.'"

Our relationship guides can be a living relative, friend, or, as in this woman's life, a parent. I believe this woman's father was working with her relationship guide to keep her from making a mistake. But there are no mistakes, and she had to learn the lesson. Usually lessons like these between husbands and wives are karmic—repayment for similar behavior in another life.

The perfect time to connect and listen to your relationship guide is when you are ending a relationship. Ask your guide about the soul lessons or karmic obligations that you had to learn from the relationship and the reasons it must end. Your guide will help you to better understand the dynamics of the agreement between the two of you. Remember that you are always learning, evolving, and expanding—that is *why you are here.*

CHAPTER 7

HEALING HELPERS

As a soul evolves, it accumulates knowledge and influences from past lives lived as it continues to strengthen its energy in an area of expertise. *Healing guides* are usually doctors, nurses, and other healers throughout many of their incarnations. They act as mentors to souls on Earth who work in similar professions. Healing helpers come in and out of our lives when we are experiencing health issues or battling addictions.

My Healing Guide

The first time I met my healing guide, I was in my weekly development circle. At the fourth meeting, we sat in our usual places and said our prayer. The lights were dim; I began to feel extremely tired, and I drifted into a half-consciousness state of mind.

When I awoke from my trance-like state, I looked around at the group and asked, "What happened?"

67

Someone said, "Don't you remember? A spirit came through you and spoke with an accent. He said his name was Harry Aldrich and that he was a doctor who lived in London at the turn of the 20th century."

Someone had taped the session, and when it was played back, I was amazed at what I sounded like. It wasn't my usual speedy pronunciation but a very elegant and sober English accent. He spoke as one would expect a doctor of that time period—with authority and self-control. He gave me advice about my health and said that he would assist me in my future work as a medium.

Dr. Aldrich has been with me ever since that unexpected event. He helps my adrenal system to properly utilize the life-force energy throughout my body. He warns me when my vitality is low or when I have accumulated too much toxic energy. The doctor assists me during my readings and demonstrations by purifying the energy around my body.

Whenever there is something physical affecting a member of my audience, Dr. Aldrich will let me know what to say. I was thrilled to know that there were helpers in the Spirit world that would be at my side not only for the dead but also for the living.

A Healer's Advice

Back in 2002 when I was in development with CBS-TV for the series *Ghost Whisperer*, I was approached by Jennifer Love Hewitt, the soon-to-be star of the show. She expressed that she was a big fan of my work and would love to have lunch with me. Several days later we enjoyed the first of many lunches together and the beginning of a lovely relationship that continued through the five seasons of the show.

In developing her character of Melinda Gordon, the woman who sees dead people, Jennifer asked if I would tutor her in the methods I use to communicate with the Spirit world. Besides teaching her the process I go through, I thought she should experience it herself and offered a reading with her mother and family. A few months later, I walked into her mom's home in the San Fernando Valley and began a session. Throughout the reading, evidential details came through from several deceased members of Jennifer's family.

But something happened that night that was very strange, even for me. Whenever I would look over at her mother I was aware that Dr. Aldrich was standing next to her wanting my attention. I know that if he shows up, there will be a message regarding the health of an individual. I listened as he spoke in his strong British accent.

He was most emphatic and insisted that Jennifer's mother's sister get a mammogram immediately as there was some imbalance in the breast tissue. To give a message like this, I had to be extremely sensitive as to not upset the recipient, yet at the same time I had to emphasize the urgency of the message.

Jennifer's mother told me she would be very happy to pass this concern on to her sister. Several weeks later on the set of the show, I visited Jennifer in her trailer. As she ran lines in her head and applied her makeup, she looked at me and shouted, "Oh my God, James! Do you remember the message your guide gave my mom about her sister?"

As with most readings, I recalled a bit of the message but not all of it. She was so excited as she spoke. "Mom told her sister about the reading, so my aunt went to the doctor and had a mammogram, and they found a malignancy. But the doctor said it was in the very early stages so it could be treated."

I was blown away when I realized that my guide Dr. Aldrich intervened to save a life. Jennifer's aunt and mom were forever grateful for the connection with Spirit and Dr. Harry's life-altering advice.

Spirit Doctors

If anyone asked me what my second passion is beside mediumship, I would have to say teaching. I find assisting others in remembering their spiritual origin and validating their intuitive abilities to be incredibly enriching, but it is the sense of freedom that people feel when they see themselves in a completely different light that is the most rewarding.

A few years back when I was teaching a five-day mediumship development course, I began the class by asking the participants why they were taking the course and what they hoped to get out of it. Many responded that they wanted to bring peace to others and felt that the healing work they could provide would be extraordinary.

As I listened to the responses, I kept looking over at one of the participants. There was a green healing energy in her aura that made her stand out from the rest. I couldn't quite figure it out until it was her turn to answer.

With frankness and compassion, Rachel explained to the class that she had spent many years working as a nurse and the last three years were at a hospice. She was an end-of-life doula and her role was to assist souls to peacefully pass to the other side. I thought hers was selfless and necessary work. I could tell she did this work without any need for appreciation or thanks, but the Spirit world had been waiting a long time for this moment.

I began to demonstrate my mediumship abilities to the students, and the first contact I made was with a spirit by the name of Jerry. He died at 78 of pneumonia. He came with Margaret, who suffered a stroke at 81. Even though they came together, they didn't seem to be connected. When I revealed this information to the students, no one related to it. So I asked my guides to be more specific and show me the person that these spirits were there for. Suddenly a little golden light appeared over Rachel's head.

Rachel did not recognize the information at first, but both spirits thanked her so much and wanted me to tell her about the butterflies. Rachel immediately understood the reference and lowered her head.

"Jerry and Margaret were two of my patients. I often tell patients to think of themselves as caterpillars turning into butterflies and flying away."

The entire class was very moved by Rachel's care for her patients. Jerry continued to say that some special people were there to be with Rachel. Immediately I became aware of three spirits—a woman dressed in the white jacket of a doctor with a stethoscope, a man who held some sort of pad, and finally a woman with a nurse's cap.

The doctor spoke first. She introduced herself as an internist and said that all three were part of Rachel's healing guides. The gentleman said he was a psychotherapist while on Earth. The other woman was a nurse who had worked in a military hospital. Rachel was very surprised to know that these beings were around her, but then she realized that when she prepared people for their journey home, sometimes thoughts would pop into her head that would be beneficial solely for the patient she was currently assisting. Rachel now understood that she had been influenced by her healing guides.

If this were not incredible enough, the doctor wanted to inform Rachel that recently they had been working with her to assist in her upset digestive system. Rachel acknowledged that she might have an ulcer. The therapist sent me a thought that he had impressed upon Rachel to see a marriage counselor. Rachel nodded. "Yes, I started seeing someone a week ago."

The healing guides continued with their message. "Your stomach issues are due to the emotional upset regarding your marriage that you are repressing," I said. "They are glad you are willing to get help and discuss your problems with a counselor." Rachel confirmed that since she had started to open communication between her and her husband, her stomach issues had begun to subside. Such an incredible message from her guides demonstrated to Rachel that they are always assisting her, not only in her healing profession but also with her personal healing.

CHAPTER 8

INSPIRATION GUIDES

Inspiration guides are evolved beings who reach out to you from the higher realms to impart higher, more esoteric, truths. Think of them as the professors of the spiritual dimensions. These beings have a greater understanding of the human condition. Inspiration guides can come in and out of our lives for brief periods—sometimes until we understand and process a troublesome spiritual conundrum.

I can always tell when my inspiration guides are around because the vibration is quickened, but they present themselves to me differently each time, depending on the inspiration. Before I wrote *Growing Up in Heaven* (a book about children who have passed on), I was in my office and began to see a whole group of spirit children running around my desk. Children are joyful guides. If they come to one of my demonstrations, I know that they are there to uplift and imbue the audience with their innocence and happiness. So after looking at these spirit children running around my office for two days, I understood that my next book would be about children.

Like everything else, inspiration is energy. And because we are energetic beings, the best way to attract your inspiration guide is to raise your energy level. We can block our energy flow by a variety of extremes such as sickness, emotional baggage, lack of sleep, too much work, and even the overuse of social media. If our minds are closed or too focused on other things, inspiration can be blocked.

Because inspirers vibrate at higher and faster frequencies, trying to get through to us when our energy is low and depleted is almost an impossible task. By raising our energy, we become channels for the higher vibrational frequencies, and ideas can flow into our minds more easily. In the last part of the book, I share some energy-raising exercises that will help with this. It's up to you to do what is necessary if you want to take advantage of the messages from your inspiration guides.

Finding Inspiration

Your inspiration guide wants you to follow your heart and be true to yourself. The road you travel may not be what others want for you, and that can be very hard to admit to yourself and to them. We are all creative, and we use our creativity to solve problems in our careers, finances, relationships, or any part of our daily lives. When we find ourselves in a difficult situation, trying to fix it with our egos can make the situation worse. We all know how that feels.

How do you become inspired? You have faith that you are not alone and that your guides and spirit friends are always around you to lend their insights. When you have faith, you will *ask for inspiration* to solve a problem and trust that the answer is forthcoming.

Inspiration guides assist us in our soul lessons by opening our energy field to include compassion, patience, understanding, and love. Many years ago I was introduced to one of my inspiration guides at a séance with world-famous British medium Leslie Flint. My guide Andre, who was once a French artist, influenced my sensitivity to the Spirit world. He also is instrumental when I am in the process of writing a book. As I'm typing this sentence, I can feel Andre nearby. Think of your inspiration guides as teachers. They will direct you, give you hints and hunches, but as always, you have to follow through.

Spiritualist Teachers

As with Leslie Flint, I have had some incredible opportunities to meet many mediums who have been walking the path for some time. Several years ago I had the privilege of meeting another one of the British old guard, Mavis Pittilla, a well-respected medium doing spiritualist work for almost 50 years. Gordon Higginson, one of the world's greatest physical mediums, was her mentor. Mavis and I became fast friends when she introduced herself to me after my first presentation in Blackpool, England. Over the years we have shared many fun and incredible times.

One of the things Mavis has said about mediumship work has always stuck with me: "I know a lot of mediums who work from the mind and not the soul. They get the information and try to work it out in their own way using the conscious mind. Whereas a soul-medium will allow the presence of spirits to communicate their own way without interference from them." It was Mavis's way of saying that we have to get our egos out of the way and let spirits speak to us in their own way. "One day people will realize that spirits are all around us and that they are intelligent and capable of saying what they want to their loved ones."

On one particular occasion, the two of us hosted a cruise to Australia. Mavis offered to sit in trance for me and show how her facial appearance changes. One evening Mavis, her partner, Jean, and I sat in my stateroom for her demonstration. Mavis closed her eyes, and in a matter of minutes, her face entirely transfigured. I could literally see the area under and around her face alter, forming a very different appearance. Her eyes appeared to widen and her cheekbones seemed higher. Even her hair looked as if it changed from gray to brown.

As I took a deep breath and closely studied the changes on Mavis's face, I noticed that she suddenly appeared much younger. I heard a gentle voice coming from Mavis. "So many things have changed since my time on Earth. I believe much progress is being made, although at times it appears things are going backwards."

I asked Jean who was speaking. Jean had seen this happen before. "It's Emma, a person from history who has always been an inspiration to Mavis." Jean could tell that I did not know who Emma was. "Emma Hardinge Britten. She lived in the 1800s and was one of the early women pioneers of the spiritualist movement." Mavis (Emma) bowed her head and smiled. "That's Emma," Jean said.

Emma let us know that she enjoyed the classes Mavis and I were teaching, and she was happy to have the opportunity to be on a cruise, something she had never experienced in her lifetime. We giggled at this last statement, and as fast as Emma had appeared, her presence left.

Afterward, I asked Mavis why the spirit was able to come in so easily. Mavis explained that she had been sitting in trance for so many years that it is easier now than it was in her early days, but now Emma has communicated through her so often, it's like slipping on a favorite glove. She completely understands the vehicle (Mavis) and how to manipulate the magnetic, energetic, and physical fields. Once Mavis was able to let go and surrender her conscious mind, it was easy for Emma to come through, although Mavis emphasizes that a part of the human mind is always present during a trance state.

I continued to ask how it seemed to be so easy to do. Mavis made it clear that because Emma had a background in spiritualism, she really understood the mechanics of physical mediumship and transfiguration. She was one of the first mediums to tour throughout the United States and educate the masses. She had written several books and, while in trance channeling the great social reformer Robert Owen, Emma received the seven principles of spiritualism that are still used today.

I am continually amazed at how we are always being watched and motivated from the other side. Our connections with our spirit teachers and other advanced beings never cease to amaze me.

An Inspirational Thinker for All Time

I have met many inspiring spirits in my years in development. I remember when I first began to sit in a development circle, there was the distinct energy of a guide in the room. I could not tell exactly who he was or what his job was, but when he was nearby—which was pretty regularly—the energy of the circle seemed stronger. I just knew this being was involved with the energetic manipulation of the space so that spirits could come closer to us.

From week to week and month to month there seemed to be some kind of experimentation with the energy. When I telepathically asked this guide to send me information about himself (he presented himself as a male energy), I would pick up bits and pieces of his personality.

I felt he was sincere and extremely bright and quite witty. His spirit seemed like that of an inventor, and on several occasions he made it clear that he would come around to inspire me with ways to look at Spirit differently. At times this guide seemed somewhat smug, as if he knew it all.

Questioning him, I asked if he had ever been on Earth, and he answered that he had. He said his work on Earth was to inspire new ideas to the masses and he was very involved in scientific observation. He did not want to relay too much about his life on Earth; he was more interested in assisting the circle to expand its sensitivity and awareness.

Because this guide primarily came through the circle, I have no recollection of his being with me on a personal basis except for the one time when I was about to write my first book. I was sitting in my office, and a quill pen that I keep on my shelf suddenly fell off. Then I heard a voice say:

My dear man, do you think that this book is truly coming from you? We are around inspiring and impressing you with words and picking up your fingers as it were to express ourselves through your hands. The words which you say you create in the physical world are indeed the end product of a long and tedious process from those of us on this side finessing thoughts and ideas for you, sir, to understand. How could you think you are doing this alone? Nothing, my friend, is ever created in the physical world that has not had its beginning first here in the mental worlds. All your great works of art, literature, poetry, and scientific inventions have their foundations in this world.

At first, this guide's message was difficult to digest because my ego thought that I was doing all the writing. I was silly to think this way because I realized that no one creates alone. All ideas and thoughts connect from the higher spheres to the lower ones.

The guide continued:

I was an author in the early formation of the Americas, so I do understand what it means to try and change another's way of thinking. This is why I understand the written word and the work you are trying to do.

I was so dumbfounded by the details of his message, I insisted the guide tell me who he was when he was alive, and he filled my mind with an incredible thought.

You may know me as Franklin. You may know me as a being instrumental in the creation of your country's Declaration of Independence.

After 18 months of sitting in a development circle, I finally had a name and an identity, and not just of anyone, but of one of the founding fathers of the United States. His words and feelings totally humbled me. From that moment on, I knew that I had the added responsibility to be a clear channel for him and many other inspirational guides who used me to bring about a change in the world's consciousness.

Inspiration guides will always influence us for our highest good. Some inspirers come from places in our universe, others from different planes of existence entirely. They may look like a shadow or a beam of light. Because we all receive in different ways, it is up to us to learn how to recognize the subtle nuances our inspiration guides present.

I sought out the help of my inspiration guides when I was formulating the next section of this book. I asked them to impart the lessons that they felt were the most important for us here on Earth to take into our daily awareness.

PART III

LESSONS FROM MY GUIDES

CHAPTER 9

ON TREATING
OTHERS

When I began formulating this section of the book, I sat in silence for about two hours and sent out the intention to my guides that I wanted some insights for my new book that I could share with readers. I didn't ask for anything specific; I just asked them what they thought were universally important lessons to share with my readers.

I thought I'd be in silence for maybe five minutes while I wrote down a few sentences. Instead what I got were flashes of memories—of readings that I had done and of events that had happened to me personally. I wrote down a synopsis of each story so I wouldn't forget it, and after the two hours were over, I asked the guides to organize the stories for me by theme. I had a clear vision of Golden Feather handing me a pen. The message was obvious: *This was to be a lesson for me as well.*

Surprisingly, once I wrote all the stories down from memory and checked my journal, it became clear how they wanted me to structure the lessons. The three lessons of this section deal with how to treat others. My guides were emphatic that this section be first because they feel that whatever belief system you create for yourself should always manifest itself with you displaying love, compassion, and respect for others. The three lessons of the subsequent chapter encourage you to be true to yourself. Each one of us has our own spiritual path—our blueprint—so no one religion or belief system is going to work for large groups of us. We are free to choose one of our own making depending on what resonates with our soul. The last chapter dealing with lessons revolves around greater truths. The lessons in this chapter deal with universal truths that my guides believe we all should adhere to while we are experiencing the physical dimension.

Lesson 1: Never Judge Another

Years ago I did a private reading that was quite a revelation. A woman came to me after the death of her mother, Helen. She explained that her mother had been an unhappy and fearful woman scarred by the fact that she had lost her family in a Nazi concentration camp from which she had barely escaped herself. For decades she lived in the shadow of the horrible experiences that she had survived in her youth.

Almost immediately, Helen's spirit came through to me. She was bursting with a message about the night she had died and conveyed the following message: "I woke up in a hospital. Very clean. Very white. And I felt very good. I thought that this must be heaven. I noticed one other bed in the room and I approached it. There was a man lying in the bed and when I got near, he opened his eyes and smiled at me. Then I recognized his face. He had been the guard at the concentration camp. I was horrified and had the overwhelming urge to put the pillow over his face. But then I realized that we were already dead."

I looked over at the daughter who was in complete shock; as was I. Helen kept on telling me her story in my head.

The man also recognized me and a tear rolled down his cheek. He wanted to tell me a story—but there was no talking. The words just appeared in my mind. He told me that he was not German, and not at the camp by choice. He said it was made clear to him that it wouldn't end well if he didn't do as he was told. He had a family back in Yugoslavia that he wanted to return to. Somehow, I was guided to forgive him, not just for his sake, but for my own soul. So I stayed with him all day, and we talked about hate and intolerance and how they poisoned our lives on Earth. I could never justify his actions, but we had come to the conclusion that we were both victims. That was when I realized I had to forgive him.

Helen had one more addition to her story.

It was only later, after I left the hospital, that I learned that the Yugoslavian man had died many, many years before me. He had volunteered to meet me in the hospital to help me heal my soul. My guide knew that I had to see both sides of our human drama before I could move on.

I told my client, "Your mother wants you to know that she is engulfed in the light of unconditional love. She is in a beautiful place now. Forgiveness has freed her from the heavy baggage she had carried in her life. She is saying, 'Let yourself love. I am in the light with all my family. I am at peace at last.'"

It's hard to imagine forgiving someone who had been so cruel and destructive, but some souls have chosen difficult incarnations that are hard for us to understand. The negative energy that we hold for them only makes us miserable. As souls, we all have value and purpose. It is natural for us to judge a person for a wrongdoing. But as Helen realized, seeing herself as a victim all her life had left her crushed and demoralized. It was only after she made peace with herself and the prison guard, who himself was a victim, that she felt free.

Lesson 2: Follow the Golden Rule

My guides have instilled in me that kindness to other beings counts much more to your spiritual evolvement than going to church weekly or tithing. It doesn't take any more time to be kind than it does to be indifferent or rude. When you express your kindness, you acknowledge that the other person deserves your light and love. You may never know how your kindness affects another. A person may be in a bind, or feeling blue, or having a hardship you don't know about, and your kindness lifts them up so they can make the correct choice.

We all know what it feels like when someone is kind to us. We appreciate the smile, the nod, or the gesture. I am in airports a lot, and someone holding a door open for me can be the greatest thing that has happened all day.

We have all heard of the term *karma*. The simple definition is whatever energy you give out you will get back, be it good or bad. The energy can take a while to return or it could happen instantly.

I was at the market once strolling the aisles when I turned the corner to see an old woman reaching for a can on a shelf that was much higher than she could reach. We were alone in the aisle and I was going to offer to help when I reached her, even though I am only a couple of inches taller. But a young, tall guy turned the corner coming from the opposite direction and, seeing her plight, sprinted to her rescue. They spoke and laughed about something; I was out of earshot, but I could tell that she was very appreciative.

About 15 minutes later I was in the checkout line next to his when the older lady pushed her cart up. When the tall guy noticed her, I could hear him say, "So we meet again!" They spoke some more even though his transaction was over. When the lady's purchases were bagged, the cashier asked her if she needed help out to her car. The woman hesitated, but the guy said to the cashier, "I'm headed in the same direction. I'd be happy to help!" And they walked off together.

The woman behind me in line said out loud, "When my mother shops alone in a store, I wish that guy could be there." *Amen*, I thought.

Lesson 3: Give Without Expectation

My husband, Brian, doesn't travel much with me anymore—he prefers to stay at home with the dogs. But one of the many trips we have taken together started on a flight to Boston from LAX for a vacation in Provincetown, Massachusetts.

The plane was pretty full, but by the time the flight attendants had closed the doors, the seat on our aisle was still empty. That meant Brian could move out of the middle seat and we could spread out. Two men across the aisle from us and one row ahead were obviously thrilled as well because the seat between them had not been taken.

Our plane stayed at the gate for a few minutes before the doors were reopened. A young woman entered and started heading down the aisle. She had a big purse, a diaper bag, and a baby with her. She was moving slowly down the aisle checking the seat numbers. I heard one of the guys opposite us say, "Please, no" under his breath. Sure enough, she stopped at their aisle, a sheepish grin on her face. Literal seconds ticked by as the three of them all looked at each other. It seemed the guys weren't going to make it easy for her.

Brian spoke up and motioned at the seat next to him. "Here, take this one. An aisle seat is probably easier for you anyway." *Shocked* is not even the word to describe the faces that stared back at us. After she computed that someone was actually being kind to her, she graciously accepted. Her purse and bag were unfortunately draped over her shoulders while she held the baby in her arms. She looked up to the overhead baggage trying to figure out where to start. Knowing that the baby had to go somewhere before she could get settled, Brian said, "I'll take her if it's okay?"

She handed Brian the baby while she got everything organized—the things she would need for the baby were kept near her, and the rest overhead. After she was seated and had the baby back in her arms, the plane took off. She thanked us and asked us what our travel plans were. She was from Boston and she gave us some good tips about sightseeing and restaurants for the couple of days we'd be there.

About an hour into the trip, the baby started to make gestures that she wanted to come over to Brian. The woman was saying, "No, sweetie, stay with Mommy." Brian said to her, "I don't mind if you don't." Let me tell you—that baby slept on Brian's chest and that woman slept in her chair until the captain came over the loudspeaker to say that we were preparing to land.

When we told our friends in Provincetown the story, the general consensus was "Holy crap! What'd you do that for?" After we returned home to California, Brian confided to me that holding that sleeping baby for four hours was one of the highlights of his trip.

CHAPTER 10

ON BEING TRUE TO YOURSELF

No one in this physical dimension knows you better than you know yourself. But so often we're willing to quantify our worth depending on other people's opinions or to let others misconstrue our kindness for weakness. My guides impressed these stories upon me to remind you that *you* created your soul's blueprint; *you* have the connection to understand your purpose in life. Why would you let someone else steer your ship?

Lesson 4: Don't Relinquish Your Power

Never be less than who you are. You are a source incarnate, a great spirit. All life is endowed with the essence of life, the oneness of all. It is part of your birthright. If you only remembered your divine selves, you would not be so quick to undermine yourself and give away your greatness. But so many have little faith in their own power or even are aware of it that they give it away and take on someone else's or find it easier to follow someone else's desires in order to replace the love they released. If you would live by your power, your troubles would melt away and you would live in the true happiness that is part of you. One must take the time to know oneself on all levels. Try to understand that you are forever a divine being and no one can ever take that away. When you remain confident in the fact that you are here for a reason, that you are important and that your feelings matter, it becomes difficult for the ego of others to marginalize you or diminish your power. Your power is life, and you are an important part of the oneness of all. The tremendous power of Spirit within you is capable of giving you a dynamic vitality that no one else could ever have, because you are a unique, distinct, individualized light of being. No one can take your freedom from you; even when you are physically withheld, your thoughts are your freedom and always your choice. Never let go of the responsibility of you and who you are and never let another take it away.

One day I was sitting down having coffee with my friend Joanie. She was a very well-known and successful businesswoman; she is self-employed and has been for the past 25 years. During our conversation we discussed how people sometimes get so caught up in a system that they forget entirely who they are and fall into a trap of being what people expect, instead of being themselves. Everything becomes so elusive. Joanie then shared with me a story about just this type of situation, which occurred in her life.

"Ever since I was a little girl," Joanie began, "I dreamed of creating commercials. I used to watch them all the time on television and would think that they were good but I could create better ones. Tons of ideas flooded through my head when I would watch a 60-second spot. I received a bachelor's degree in advertising and marketing, and after graduation I took a job in Manhattan at one of the top ad agencies in the country. I was the assistant to one of the copywriters there named Paul.

"I was so desperate to be accepted and for Paul to see my worth that I said 'yes' to everything he threw at me. I never turned anything down. I rewrote all his copy, gave him a ton of ideas, and even ended up picking out his shirts and ties for business meetings. I just wanted to be 'seen' and acknowledged. Throughout my first year there, I took home large amounts of work, babysat large accounts, and made tons of excuses for Paul's indiscretions.

"I remember in the second year of my employment, there was a woman named Mary Ellen who started working at the firm that Paul was very romantically interested in. The only problem was that he was married. Paul wanted to get closer to her, so I managed his schedule so that they would be at the same places together. The relationship flourished and in a short while the company found out about the affair and everything came crashing down. The execs investigated Paul and even found him lying about various accounts he was working on privately. Paul blamed everything, including his meet-up with Mary Ellen, on me. Eventually the company took his word and I became the scapegoat. Security literally escorted me out of the building.

"I was gone and was never able to get another job in advertising. I was so hurt and angry. I went on for years blaming Paul for all the bad things that happened in my life from that point on. I thought he was responsible for everything until one day when I got tired of blaming and thought, *Maybe my life would be better if I took responsibility for my own actions and honored myself for who I was, not who*

I thought the world wanted me to be. I am successful and loving myself just the way I am.

"I tell you James, the moment I became aware of the words I used on a daily basis and took back my power, not letting other people's opinions matter anymore, my life really took off. I had so many interested companies, I ended up turning down jobs! The moment I accepted *me* for *me*, I became alive."

I gave Joanie a hug and said, "You did the right thing. It was a lesson in courage. You weren't meant to stay there. You were guided to go in a different direction. Each of us learns lessons in different ways. Some lessons are harder than others, especially when we are giving it our all."

The role you have decided to play in life is vital. Never let someone tell you how to live your life. When you relinquish your uniqueness to make someone else happy, you are doing a disservice not only to yourself but to the Universe. Don't be so quick to undermine your abilities or justify your beliefs. Insecurity stems from a fragile ego. Be true to yourself and express who you are.

It is important that you take the necessary steps to make the journey of self-love and self-discovery. Otherwise, how can you love another if you have not loved yourself first? Remember that the more you believe about yourself, the more you become that person.

One of the ways we can learn about ourselves is by expressing our feelings. All our feelings are valid. Our job is to look at them without judgment and ask ourselves, what purpose does this serve? Even if your feelings are silly or inconsequential, they are manifesting for a reason. The key to expressing yourself is to release your feelings without harm to another. If you stop the flow of your energy by stuffing down your self-expression, the energy becomes blocked and can turn into aggression and dis-ease.

Lesson 5: Your Beliefs Are Right for You

Recently I flew from Newark, New Jersey, across the country to San Diego, a trip I do very often when returning from teaching and lecturing at various venues on the East Coast. During the trip, the flight attendant began the process of asking the passengers about their dinner selections. As she asked each person, she checked her manifest and called everyone by name. When she left, the man next to me looked over and asked, "Hey, you're James Van Praagh, the guy who talks to dead people?" Being very tired from a long week of work, I humorously responded, "And occasionally the living."

"My name is Danny." Danny began to tell me a little about himself. He was 34 and serving in the Coast Guard. He said that for the past several years he has been studying about various religions and belief systems. *Well*, I thought, *this could be an interesting seatmate.* So I asked him, "Have you come to any conclusions?" Danny then revealed his true colors. "I was joking," he said. "I don't believe in any of it and I don't believe in what you do. I just put on an act to see your reaction."

I was taken aback by his unexpected impertinence. I wondered, *How am I going to spend the next five hours sitting next to this person?* Just as quickly, I realized that my guides would not have put me in this position if they didn't have a plan. So I had two choices—I could respond emotionally, or be civil. I chose the latter for the time being.

When I asked Danny if he had ever seen me work, he replied smugly, "No, don't need to. I know many kinds of 'cold-reading techniques.' People are stupid to believe in a god, an afterlife, or anything that keeps them from living the one life they have."

I asked him, "When you say *god*, what do you mean by that?" He shrugged his shoulders and replied, "You know, the old guy up in the clouds who wrote the Bible."

"Ah," I said. "I don't believe in that either."

Danny snickered. "What, then? Zeus, Thor, the flying spaghetti monster?"

"Nope, not them either," I said, shaking my head. "I don't believe in any deity."

Danny thought he had me cornered. "You know what that makes you, right? An atheist!"

"Technically, I am. But that doesn't mean I can't believe in a soul or the afterlife. I can construct any belief system that makes me happy, as long as that belief system encourages me to care about others and not pass judgment."

Danny was a smart guy and knew that I was alluding to our introduction. "Yeah, but I still don't like people like you who fill everybody's heads with things that haven't been proven."

"I don't think I *fill people's heads*," I said. "I just say what I believe and people are free to believe it or not. It's not my place to tell anyone what I think is right or wrong for them."

I think Danny was getting tired of the conversation because he chose instead to watch a movie. I certainly had no expectations of Danny to mellow, but after his movie was over, he removed his headphones and tapped me on the shoulder.

"Hey, James, sorry I was a jerk earlier. Just because we have different viewpoints doesn't give me the right to be mean." I accepted his apology and for the rest of the trip, we had a pleasant conversation.

I believe that everyone has a right to believe the way they choose, and we should honor their choice. All of us are the result of our life experiences and the way we were taught. Being rude, calling people names, making fun of someone—they are all part of the ego's need to attack, blame, deflect, and project.

There is no such thing as a wrong or right belief system. Accept the teachings that resonate with you. Every soul is on a different path, but our paths are on the same map. Eventually, all roads lead home. Follow the route that speaks to your heart.

Lesson 6: Be Yourself

Although we live in an imperfect world, we are perfect souls created by divine design. If you look at nature, you will see that rocks, trees, flowers, water, mountains, and so forth come in a number of varieties. No one could even try to design the beauty of nature. Think of yourself as part of nature and perfectly designed just the way you are. If you hide your true identity because you are afraid others will make fun of you, you dim your light. Even as a little boy, I understood that I had to be myself despite the fact that other kids called me "different" and "weird."

When speaking to my guides about this lesson, I was reminded of my friend Olivia, who definitely marched to the beat of her own drum. She never was one to shy away from her uniqueness. Her inquisitive mind made our time together special. People often thanked Olivia for being her delightfully quirky self. She had a special sense of humor and a fearlessness about life that everyone found appealing.

I met Olivia about 30 years ago through my friend Sarah Stevenson. Sarah, Olivia, several others, and I formed a development circle, and we sat together once a week for several years. During that time, Olivia, Sarah, and I became close; the three of us would spend many hours discussing philosophy and our views of the Spirit

world. You might say that we were all on a spiritual journey together sharing our insights and experiences.

Away from the circle, we were always ready and willing to meet with other like-minded individuals. I remember the time we had the privilege of sitting with physical
medium Leslie Flint. Leslie used an apparatus known as
an ectoplasmic voice box that enabled discarnate spirits
to speak through him. People who knew the spirits said
that they sounded exactly like the people they were when
they were alive. I distinctly recall a spirit voice speaking
to Olivia and calling her "a strange card!" We all laughed
because Olivia was exactly that, and it was incredible
to have someone from the other side validate what we
all knew.

Olivia had no problem expressing herself. She lived by
her own rules and was constantly on a quest of discov-
ery and exploration. She wanted to know the reasons why
people acted the way they did and would go out of her way
to find out. To say she was unconventional is putting it
mildly. She would often tell me, "I have to be myself." She
certainly knew no other way. To hang out with Olivia was
indeed a pleasure. We would find the most trivial of things
completely hilarious.

I remember the time I was driving her home early on
a Saturday evening. As we headed down her street, we
noticed a neighbor's home all lit up for what seemed like a
party. Olivia told me to stop and park the car. I could see
she was mesmerized by the crowd of people walking into
the house.

She looked at me and said, "Do you want to go?" I
responded, "But we don't know anyone." Olivia shrugged
me off as she got out of the car. "Everybody knows somebody," she screeched as she made a beeline for the house.
"If anyone asks, just tell them you're a friend of Mike."

ON Being True to Yourself

I could not believe that we were crashing a party, but I was caught up in the thrill of Olivia's sense of fun and adventure. The door was open, so we casually strolled in. There were about 40 or more people circulating around the living room. On one side there was a huge buffet table. Since we hadn't eaten all day, we quickly grabbed plates and started to dive in. As we dished ourselves some lovely pasta and vegetables, a young woman standing next to Olivia started to make small talk. "Isn't this a lovely party?" the woman asked Olivia. "Who do you know here?"

In her inimitable style, Olivia did not miss a beat. She beamed a smile and answered, "Oh, Mike and I are good friends." The woman responded, "Are you?" Olivia kept up the act, "Oh, yes, for years!" The woman smiled back. "How great! Mike spilled something on his shirt and had to change. He just dashed upstairs for a minute. I'm sure he'll want to say hello."

Olivia wasn't expecting that reply, so I interjected, "Great! It will be good to see him; it's been a long time." Olivia bumped into me with her plate and cocked her head to the side signaling we should eat and run. So we did just that. We went to the backyard, sat at a picnic table, and ate quickly. We were underneath an open window and we heard someone say, "Mike, go get yourself a new plate of food, and be careful this time!"

That was our cue to leave through the side gate and hightail it to the car, where we howled with laughter. Never in a million years would I have *thought* to crash the party, much less actually do it. But free-spirited Olivia didn't set limits on herself. More than anyone else, she knew what God had created her to be, so she lived it. Anything else would seem sacrilegious to her.

97

Because Olivia was one of my closest friends, we made a pact that whoever got to the Spirit world first would let the other one know immediately and share the experience. Alas, it became apparent that Olivia would be the first. She suffered a stroke that impeded her movement and speech, but not her wit. Her mind still worked at a mile a minute, but her body couldn't keep up. It was very frustrating for her. She was miserable.

As I was driving my car last summer, Olivia popped into my head. I heard her say, *Well, I am out of the body at last! I'm here to let you know.* I sent her a thought, *Did you pass? When did it happen?* I heard her response loud and clear, as if she were speaking to me on the phone. *Today!* And then she was gone.

Two hours later, I got back home and checked my e-mails. Sure enough, there was one from Olivia's daughter informing me that her mother passed away that day! I looked to the heavens and smiled. "Good-bye, my dear friend."

Olivia came to me in a subsequent meditation. I asked her to hold on as I switched my phone to *record*, and then I repeated her words.

I must say it is quite amazing. I thought at first I was dreaming because I knew I had fallen asleep in bed. The first people I saw were my father, brother, and even a grandfather whom I hadn't seen in over 60 years. It was very strange. I kept asking them, Did I die? If I did, I felt wonderful. I was greeted by so many people—some I knew, and others I didn't. But I knew that in some way I had touched each and every one of them, even those with whom I had the briefest contact.

I didn't realize how much I have helped or hurt people until I came here. You have to be careful of the thoughts and words you use, as they are very real. When I asked someone how they knew me, they projected a memory like a picture playing in my mind. Even when I asked someone how I knew them, they told me to look in my mind for a memory, and it appeared in my mind as if I were looking at a home movie.

Death is but a return home, like going back to who you really are but have forgotten. It feels as if I was in suspended animation when I lived on Earth. When I walk here, flowers come to life in all their beauty and majesty. This place is truly a reflection of your soul.

And you James, my friend, I can truly say that you were my guide on Earth. Thank you for helping me to see the rings of life and learn about the light world.

I was so amazed by Olivia's message, I had to ask her a practical question. She answered in true Olivia fashion. *Did you meet Sam Francis yet?* Sam Francis was a famous artist whom Olivia and I knew very well. Olivia worked for him for a year, and as payment he promised a painting that he would do just for her. Unfortunately, before he could make good on that promise, he passed away from prostate cancer in 1994. When she told me about her reunion in Spirit with him, I fell on the floor laughing.

Yes, I saw Sam. He handed me a painting, and I looked at him and said—a lot of good it does me now. Thanks, but no thanks!

Olivia didn't lose her unique perspective and personality. It goes to show that expressing our uniqueness is to be celebrated. Who knows how your expression can assist others along their journey. So many of us feel the need to conform, even if it means inhibiting the natural qualities of our own personalities. I've been guilty of that, but I was blessed to know someone like Olivia who not only followed her own path, she blazed her trail.

CHAPTER 11

ON GREATER TRUTHS

Lesson 7: Accept Struggles as Lessons

A little boy I knew felt very singled out and angry that God had given him a big tumor that began to grow underneath his jaw. He was a good boy—an altar boy!—so why did this happen to him? He knew lots of kids who deserved a tumor more than he did. Especially the kids who bullied him at school because he was so short. The growth on his neck now made him even more vulnerable to his classmates' ridicule. At nine years old, the injustice didn't make sense.

After a battery of tests and what seemed like an endless line of doctors pawing at the little boy's neck, his parents decided that the best thing to do was to allow an operation to remove the tumor.

Early one Monday morning, his mother drove him to the Manhattan Eye, Ear and Throat Hospital in New York City. Unlike the little boy, most of the kids in the children's ward were there to get their tonsils removed.

His mother got him settled and she stayed until visiting hours were over. As she kissed him good-bye, she said, "You be a strong little soldier for me."

His room was more like a ward—there were several beds and the kids were allowed to socialize and play. But none of the other children wanted to play with the strange little boy with the lump on his neck. The boy became very sad and depressed and didn't understand why the other children were so mean to him. He felt very alone.

As he sat at the play table by himself, his emotions took over and he began to cry. "Why are you crying?" a voice asked. He looked up and sitting next to him was another little boy who introduced himself as Frankie. He explained to Frankie about how the other children teased him because he looked so different. Frankie said, "Oh, what do they know? I think your lump is cool. It shows you have so much niceness inside, it has to burst out. Why don't you think of yourself as some kind of superman with special powers?" The little boy smiled and asked his new friend, "Why are you here?" Frankie told him, "I hurt my ear by sticking a pencil in it." And the two boys laughed out loud. Little by little, other kids would start to trickle over and play. Frankie had made it okay.

Early the next morning, the little boy went into surgery. When he woke up, he began to throw up violently. Groggy from the anesthetic he was given, he looked around and didn't know where he was. Then he felt the huge bandage around his neck, and he remembered.

Later that morning, his first desire was to show Frankie his bandage, but he discovered that his friend was already gone. One by one, all the other children who had come to accept him were being discharged, and a new group were admitted for their upcoming tonsillectomies. He started to feel very self-conscious about the big bandage covering one side of his face. After the new children were finally settled in and all the parents were gone, the children started to assess each other. His bandage got a few lingering looks but most of the interest was devoted to a boy who had something wrong with his mouth. The top lip didn't come together and a scar ran from his lip all the way up into his nose, which also was kind of crooked.

At first the boy with the bandage felt a sense of relief that someone was taking the attention away from him, but he could tell that the boy with the funny lip was unhappy and frightened. He recalled that same look in himself when Frankie had first approached him. He knew what he must do.

He walked over to where the little boy with the lip sat on his bed. "Hi, my name is Jamie Van Praagh. What's yours?"

After I was discharged from the hospital, my mother took me to the top of the Empire State Building. I remember riding the crowded subway and feeling so small among the giant adults who pushed and jostled to get a seat. When we lined up in the lobby to ride the elevator to the top, I could barely contain my excitement. I clutched my mother's hand as we entered the elevator and squeezed into the small space with so many people. As we sped to the top, I could feel my stomach drop and my mother's grip tightened.

When the doors opened on the outdoor observatory deck, I ran to the railing and looked out. I had never seen anything like it—the whole city before my eyes and everything looked like tiny specks. I was struck by the silence; the noise and clamor of the city below was far off. There was only blue sky dotted with clouds above me. It was so beautiful that I didn't want to leave, but eventually my mother grabbed my hand and we walked to another side.

Seeing the city from above shifted my perspective. I had the sense that from this vantage point that I was privy to everything that was going on below me. I was seeing what I call now *the bigger picture*. My mind drifted back to my stay in the hospital. I could sense an unseen hand teaching me a valuable lesson. As much as I felt personally targeted by God for giving me that tumor in the first place, now that the ordeal was over, I felt it was a gift. I was fine and healthy now, but I was left with the beautiful lesson of empathy.

Whenever I feel crowded and pushed by people or events, my mind goes back to that scene on the observation deck, and the bigger picture comes into focus. I look at the scar under my neck, and I think of it as my badge of courage. I wear it with pride and happiness because it was a test, and I passed that test. I never gave in to negativity and instead found the power within to love myself and share my love with others.

Lesson 8: Thoughts Create Your Reality

Everything in the physical dimension is a thought come to life. We are in the driver's seat with the ability to design our lives the way we want. Projecting our fears and insecurities onto other people creates a reality of fear and insecurity where it may not exist. Each of us is a creator. It is our responsibility to make conscious, healthy choices. Feeling joy is your true expression as a spiritual being. We can get so caught up in everyday annoyances that we forget that within our soul's creative makeup is the element of joy that can be used to balance the flow of energy and create harmony.

I live in San Diego County, a home to many senior citizens. We are fortunate to enjoy Southern California's incredible weather, good food, and unique sense of freedom. But there are drawbacks, and driving the freeways is probably the most prominent of all. Sometimes it takes the strangest of circumstances to bring out our joyous selves, and I was a witness to this recently.

I had a meeting scheduled in Los Angeles, and several friends suggested that I take the train as it would be easier than driving the dreaded San Diego Freeway. Following their advice, I bought a ticket for the two-hour train ride headed north. I got on the train and sat there for at least 15 minutes. As the minutes ticked by, I wondered if this was a normal occurrence. Suddenly my attention was drawn to a commotion taking place on the platform.

As I looked out the window, I saw a female station agent helping an old man walk toward the train. The agent was carrying a pet crate. They boarded the car I was in, and I watched as the agent got the old man and his dog situated two rows in front of me. The courteous agent was now gushing over how cute she thought the dog was. The old man cut her short and said, "You can leave us now. I just don't want to be bothered or fussed over." Taken aback, the agent quickly took her leave.

Finally the train left the station and we were on our way. Not long into the trip, the dog began to whimper. I could hear a woman sitting near the old man say, "I'm sure no one here cares if you want to let your dog out and hold him."

The man snapped back, "He's fine in there. He doesn't like strangers. You'd only scare him." With that, the woman backed off.

I thought, *poor guy,* and questioned my decision to take what was going to be a long train ride. As the train chugged along northbound, I gazed over at the man from time to time and caught him falling in and out of sleep. I began wondering how a person could get to the point of being so closed off from obvious charitable acts, when I became aware of three spirit children encircling him. I had the sense that the children were not related to the man; instead, they seemed to be guides sent with the specific purpose of inspiring a gentle lightness and joy in this troubled soul.

As I peered over to watch these gleeful children, the dog (obviously sensing the guides) began barking uncontrollably. Still half-asleep, the old man waved his hand to stop the dog from barking. I sent a telepathic message to the guides, asking about their intentions. I was told that the man loved the dog so much that he wouldn't travel without it. He was ashamed to think that people would judge that as a weakness, and that people would be upset that a dog would be on the train with them.

I understood what the guides were saying: The old man had created a reality for himself even before he got on the train. He had put walls and barriers up around him with his thoughts, hoping to be left alone because he was expecting judgment when none would have existed if it weren't for his behavior. If he hadn't created the current atmosphere with his own preconceived thought, his experience on the train would be much happier. The guides were telling me that they were working on his mind-set.

A girl of about 10 years of age walked up the aisle from behind me and stopped in front of the old man. "Mister," she said, "I brought some water for your dog," as she placed a bowl of water at his feet.

"That's okay," he said, "she doesn't need it. Thanks anyway."

"But I brought it for her. Can we try?"

The man looked around at the other passengers and seemed to be embarrassed. He opened the crate and brought out a little dachshund and put it on the ground. The dog drank some water and wagged its tail. The little girl laughed and said, "What's her name?"

"Doxie," he told her as his eyes scanned the other passengers warily.

"Can I hold her?" the girl asked.

"Sure," he replied.

The girl picked Doxie up and received some kisses. The girl squealed with delight and the old man smiled for the first time. When Doxie was put back down, she immediately dashed away to investigate all the other people.

"Doxie, no!" he yelled. But Doxie was already making new friends. Doxie greeted everyone, including me. I could hear people saying "Hi, baby" and "You're so cute." I could actually see the panic and fear disappear from the old man's face as people looked over to him and smiled. In response, the man began to cry, realizing that people are indeed good and that he doesn't need to shut them out.

It was a very special journey, and the beautiful spirit guides did an astounding job at exposing the grumpy old man to the simple joy of sharing with another. As the train passed by Long Beach station, I heard him tell a fellow passenger how this was not the first time Doxie "saved his life." He hugged Doxie. It was apparent that Doxie was also the old man's guide because she certainly brought out the best in him.

Like the man on the train, we can keep to ourselves feeling separated and alone, or we can reach out to others. People are always willing to help because everyone is light. Some let their light shine more brightly than others. It is our job to recognize the light in one another and encourage that light to glow.

Lesson 9: Stay Open-Minded

When my guides reminded me of this next story, at first I thought the lesson was about staying open-minded to the messages around us. But when the memory continued, I realized that it was also about being open to new ways of thinking and not dismissing evidence just because it doesn't fit into your paradigm.

It was the late 1990s, and my book *Talking to Heaven* was still on the charts. I was living in L.A. and Brian would drive 90 minutes north from Orange County every weekend after he got off work. This particular Friday, I had just returned home from a trip where I had laid out on the beach and got sunburned. As Brian was putting some aloe vera on my back, I said, "This reminds me of that movie where Charles Grodin goes on his honeymoon and his wife gets a bad sunburn."

Brian stopped cold. "I can't believe you're saying that! Just at work today, someone who knows that I'm good with movie trivia asked me the name of the movie where Charles Grodin falls in love with Cybill Shepherd when he's on his honeymoon! What are the chances *The Heartbreak Kid* would come up twice in one day?"

We laughed it off and continued our normal Friday routine of grabbing something to eat and then going to the video store for a movie to watch. This was back in the day when you used to have to go to a store and rent a VHS if you wanted to watch a movie at home. Anyway, we made our selection and waited in line to pay for it. The woman ahead of us was called to the counter and we could hear her say to the clerk, "I rented this movie yesterday but when I tried to play it, it didn't work. I don't know if something is wrong with the tape or with my VCR." The clerk popped the VHS into his machine behind the counter—and, I kid you not—the opening credits of *The Heartbreak Kid* appeared on the screen.

Brian and I looked at each other wide-eyed. I thought maybe I was on *Candid Camera* or *Punk'd*. We spent the rest of the weekend wondering what my guides were trying to let me know. On Monday morning I received a call from the producers of *The Charles Grodin Show* (he was beginning a talk show on cable); they wanted me to appear on a segment about the paranormal. So, mystery solved.

But the second lesson didn't happen until we were recording the show. I was scheduled to be on with my friends Dr. Brian Weiss and John Edward, as well as a skeptic that these TV shows always feel obligated to have on in order to seem "fair and balanced." John did a phone reading for a random caller during which he asked her, "Does August 14 mean something to you?" The caller responded, "Yes, that's my birthday!" Everyone on the panel thought that was an excellent hit—except the skeptic. When Charles asked him why he didn't think it was amazing, the skeptic said, "If he had said to the caller 'Your birthday is August 14,' that would be miraculous. But he didn't. He said, 'Does August 14 mean something to you?' There are lots of people who have August 14 as a birthday."

The panel actually laughed at him until we realized that he was dead serious. He wouldn't budge an inch; his mind was closed to the possibility that John had picked up the caller's birthday over the phone. We tried to be very gracious and just agree to disagree, but that was the moment I knew I would no longer care about naysayers. I was just going to do my thing, and whatever they thought about me was none of my business.

PART IV

CONTACTING
YOUR GUIDES

CHAPTER 12

TRAINING YOUR MIND

The life that we see is but a sliver of our actual reality. And the body that you look at in a mirror contains but a sliver of your soul. The energy of your Higher Self is woven into the fabric of all that there is. It is in all places at all times. The part of your soul that is participating in this physical dimension—the part that is reading this sentence right now—has volunteered to focus its awareness in this limiting, instructive, dense arena that we call Earth. But you are so much more.

Think of your soul as a sun emanating infinite rays of light. Your "present" life is one of these rays, but this ray has chosen to only be aware of itself. In reality, the *totality of you* is experiencing other dimensions and lifetimes, embarking on great endeavors and small tasks, processing great emotions of love and loss. But all rays are feeding the whole. You—this one ray that you are aware of—have purpose and you are integral to the welfare of your Higher

Self. I want to help train your mind so that you can begin to tap into the other dimensions of your soul. When you shift your awareness away from your lower mind, or ego, you will give your guides and spirit loved ones the space to bring their influences into your own soul. Remember that your mind is not your brain and it is not inside your body. The higher mind of which I am speaking is your soul, and it exists in realms far beyond what the human brain can understand.

The most important key in expanding your awareness is to know yourself. For although it is true that we are all one, here on Earth we have the illusion of separateness. It is foreign and odd for our soul to feel separated and isolated, but these are the conditions that we have agreed to when choosing to incarnate in the physical. But here's the good part: When you work hard at knowing who you are, it is easier for you to recognize what is *other* than you. This is called discernment.

Just as a toddler learns from his parents what is right and wrong, our guides help us navigate this difficult dimension by impressing their wisdom on us. We just have to train ourselves to be open to their insights.

Preliminary Ground Rules

I can't stress enough how important I believe it is to keep a spiritual journal to track your progress. Begin by writing down your reasons and expectations for contacting your guides. After you get your journal, hold it with your intention, such as: *In this journal, I will keep the information my guide gives me.* You can name it "My Guide Book" or "Wisdom from My Spirit Guides," just like the title of this book.

It is important that you set aside a time each day (the same time if possible) to center yourself in your heart (soul center). In the next chapter, I will be giving you advice on how to raise your energy so you will be more receptive to Spirit. You want to show the Spirit world that you are a serious student.

Set your daily intention. Remember, it is very important that you let Spirit know why you want to communicate with it. You may want to serve others, or you may want to find out the lessons you came into this life to learn. Make sure your ego is not in the way. Let your intention come from your heart.

Take the time to create a reference or symbolic library. Spirit often communicates with symbols, and it is imperative that you have established what each symbol represents. For instance, a ring can symbolize marriage or the intention to marry. A rose can be an apology or a romantic gesture. Every person who intends to contact Sprit should establish a reference code, and your journal is a great place to write this down until deciphering the symbols becomes second nature. Write as many references/associations as you can concerning earthly milestones that will assist you when communicating with your guides.

You are a spirit first and foremost, so remember, it is from your own sense of divinity that you will be communicating with your guides. It has nothing to do with the human part of you. You need to remember that any time that you come from a place of judgment, it is your ego getting in the way. Most Earth situations are benign to Spirit; they simply exist. It is the human ego that puts labels like "good," "bad," and "wrong" on things. It will take time, so above all *please be patient* with the process. I have been doing this for more than 30 years, and I am still learning.

Set Your Intention

From the moment you wake up every day, you must have a sense of gratitude. *Thank you for giving me another day to learn.* Be mindful of your thoughts. I know that a lot of you who are reading this are thinking, *My body is in constant pain. I should be grateful for that?* Or *My child has died. I'm supposed to be happy?* I don't want to sound like I'm trivializing your battles or that I don't have empathy for your struggles. What I'm saying is that it's my belief that obstacles have been placed in our paths so we can learn from them. In my worldview, everything in the physical dimension is temporary; it is your soul that is perfect and immortal. Try not to drag yourself out of bed each morning and think negatively. Also, don't walk around in a daze. Train yourself to become constantly aware and conscious. Thoughts are real—they can affect your mood *and* your health.

When you take a shower and the water flows over you, close your eyes and for a moment picture a golden light of loving energy flowing into your body. Be aware that you are receiving this golden light in every cell, muscle, bone, and tissue. See the light expand and flow through your energy field and beyond your body into your spiritual self. As it does, imagine all energies that are not for your highest good dissolve and flow down the drain. Mother Earth will neutralize those. This golden light brings you a sense of balance, peace, and connection to the One Source. In complete awareness you know that you are part of the Universe, and that this beautiful energy stays with you throughout the day.

As you are preparing to leave the shower, say, "May God go before me and show me the way today." You are setting your intention and programming the spaces you will encounter each day. When you send out this thought, you're actually transmitting that vibration and the same energy will return to you. Make your intention personal to you. I vary my intentions throughout the week. Sometimes I say, "I am a magnet. I will attract only love and the experiences that are for my highest good." Or: "Spirit, guide me today. May everybody who comes upon my path be enlightened."

Set your intention daily. Make it a habit. If you have to, put a note or object in or near the shower to remind you to invoke your intention. In two weeks, you will start to feel centered, connected, and balanced. You will have a sense of renewal.

Shifting Your Awareness

A huge percentage of our conscious awareness is devoted to the material world. It's not our fault—it's a necessity. We have to be aware of our surroundings in this physical dimension. We have to be attuned to our five senses all the time. We have to watch where we're going or what our kids or pets are doing; we have to listen to people talking or be aware of sirens while driving; we need to be able to smell smoke or gas; we need to detect if food has gone bad, or if something is too hot or sharp to touch. For most of us, we neglect or forget to shift our awareness from the physical to the spiritual. Since we *are* spiritual beings temporarily having a physical experience, it seems like the amount of time we spend navigating Earth versus nurturing our spirit is imbalanced. I think it's appropriate that we start to shift some of our awareness to our real home turf.

This brings us to the subject of meditation. I can't stress enough how instrumental a daily meditation ritual is for anyone who wants to contact their guides. I have written a special guided meditation for you in the last chapter of this book to assist you with that. But to help you feel comfortable with your awareness being outside of your physical body, I have a couple of exercises for you here.

Psychic Travel

Pick a time of day when you're least likely to be disturbed. Find a comfortable spot and close your eyes. Take a few deep breaths in and out to center yourself. Now let your awareness leave your physical body and let it wander out of the room. As you are still physically seated with your eyes closed, let your consciousness examine an adjoining room. Take in every detail. What is on the floor? A stray sock? A toy? A pair of shoes? What is on the tabletops? Is there a coffee mug? A pair of eyeglasses? A set of keys?

Let your awareness drift out the front door. Look up in the sky. Are there clouds? What is the weather like? What is the position of the sun or moon? Are there any cars parked in the street? What color are they? Are there any leaves on the ground? Can you count them? Take your time.

Slowly let your awareness come back into your body. Take a few deep breaths and open your eyes. When you're ready, go and check to see if you were correct. Don't be discouraged if you weren't. You'll only get better with practice. As you get more comfortable with the exercise, start to expand your psychic travels.

Word of the Day

In the morning, find an object in your home (or outside in the yard, if possible) that catches your attention. It could be a flower, a leaf, a rock—anything that calls to you. Touch or hold the object and close your eyes. Take a few deep breaths to center yourself. As you caress the object, send out a thought to Spirit. Ask your guide to telepathically send you one word. Once you get the word, go back inside.

Throughout the day, be aware when the word shows up in your travels. You may be driving your car when you see the word on a billboard. Or someone says the word on the radio. You may be at work when the word comes up in a meeting. Pay attention to how often this word shows up. Also be aware if the object is mentioned. For instance, if you held a flower, someone may receive a bouquet. At the end of the day, go to your object and focus on it once again. Ask your spirit guide: What did I have to learn about this word? Was there a lesson in that word for me?

Practice these two exercises on a regular basis. Shifting your awareness is a process that doesn't happen overnight. However, once you establish your connection to the Spirit lands, you will attract beings that will help and guide you.

Opening the Channel

Once you start having success with your psychic abilities within our own dimension, it's time to try some interdimensional exercises. Remember, the Spirit world is not a different place than where we are. Our existences are interwoven and intertwined. Laws of physics don't allow our physical bodies to travel outside of our Earth dimension, but our conscious energy certainly can. And, although spirits are free to cross the boundary, we can assist them by opening a channel to receive messages. These exercises will help you to tune into the awareness of the Spirit world around you. Be sure to have your spirit journal handy.

Spirit Memory

Close your eyes and become aware of your breathing. Gently breathe in and out. As you breathe in, visualize love coming into you, and as you breathe out, release fears, limitations, expectations, upsets, and any negativity you may be holding onto. Breathe in through your nose for a count of four and out through your mouth for a count of four. In a sense, you are breathing in your soul and breathing out your ego. Become aware of the space above your head and the space below your feet. Do this exercise slowly for about 10 minutes while thinking of all your loved ones who have made the transition to the Spirit realms.

At the top of the page in your journal, write down the name of a loved one who has passed over. Then close your eyes and gently breathe in and out as you did in the exercise above. After a few minutes, imagine the color green around your heart. Think of an occasion you two attended that has special significance. Remember as many details as you can: What were you wearing? What time of year was it? What kind of mood were you in? When you are ready, send a thought to your loved one. Ask them to tell you about their experience at that occasion. Listen to their point of view about that memory. Let them tell you anything and everything. When you are ready, open your eyes and write down the message from your loved one.

The Mirror

Stand or sit in front of a mirror so you can see your face. If you can dim the lights, that would be ideal. Stare into the mirror as you begin your breathing exercise to center yourself. Keep your eyes open and look into them. See yourself as a spirit being—one that is temporarily using a physical body. Understand that you are surrounded by spirit beings at all times. These are your loved ones who no longer inhabit a physical shell. Feel their presence. Close your eyes and ask someone from the Spirit world to come closer, perhaps just above your head. Maintain a clear, steady image of your loved one's face right above your head.

Slowly open your eyes, still holding the image firm. Are you able to manifest your loved one in the mirror? Be patient. Ask the spirit to come closer and actually meld with your energy. Be aware of any sensations that seem different than your own. Invite your loved one to use your loving energy to communicate. Have a conversation. When the contact becomes weak, it is time to let them go. Release them with love. Slowly breathe in and out as you come back to your physical surroundings. Be sure to write down the conversation in your journal.

Experience the Spirit Space

Unless you graduated college with a science degree, you probably don't understand much about energy waves. I don't, either. Sound waves, microwaves, radio waves, X-rays, radar—I just take for granted that they exist without knowing how they work. The same is true with the energy—or soul—of someone or something that doesn't currently inhabit a physical vessel. I can't deny that I receive information from beings who are outside of my personal awareness; I just can't tell you how it happens scientifically. But what helps me is to imagine—in human terms—*how* it enters my consciousness. These are techniques that I used in my own development as a medium. Be sure to have your journal with you.

Sacred Place

Close your eyes and center yourself with your breathing exercise. When you are ready, become aware of the space above you. Visualize a golden light that is wide at the top and narrows, like a funnel, near the top of your head. Examine this space with your concentrated awareness. This space is not part of your physical body, but it is part of your sacred space. It belongs to you and you are in control of what enters.

Once you feel comfortable, project your entire body into this space, as if your feet are planted on top of your own shoulders. Feel what it is like in the atmosphere above your head. What does the energy feel like there? This is where spirit energy and your conscious mind meet. Become familiar with this space because you're going to spend a lot of time here. Try not to let your ego interfere by asking a lot of unnecessary questions. Keep centered and explore the energy. The more you know about this space and feel this atmosphere, the more your mind can explore, and the easier it is for spirit guidance to come to you.

When you're ready, slowly come back into your own body. In your journal, write down a list of words that describe this space. Is it peaceful, comforting, beautiful, light, dark, empty, etc.? Do you feel at home there? What changes would you like to make on your next visit? This is a place where you—and Spirit—need to feel comfortable. Make it special.

We Haven't Met

Close your eyes and center yourself with your breathing exercise. Think about your family tree and pick out a relative who you never met or knew personally. For instance, this relative could have died before you were born or when you were an infant. It might be a grandparent, aunt, uncle, cousin—someone in your family you know little about. Ask this person to enter the sacred space above your head. Greet them lovingly. Take notice of their appearance and demeanor. Do they seem shy as they greet you or demonstrative? Funny or serious? Invite them to share information with you.

Ask them to discuss different periods in their life such as their family life, interests, hobbies, work, goals, experiences, as if they are giving you a biography. Let them fill your mind with as much information as they can give. Remember to always let your ego step aside. Don't assist spirits by telling them about themselves. Let this spirit merge with you so that you know all about his or her life. When the spirit's energy leaves, open your eyes and write the details in your journal. If possible, ask a family member about this loved one to see if any of the information is accurate.

Opening yourself up to the Spirit world is like learning a different language. It takes time and practice. Don't be discouraged by setbacks. And don't compare yourself to others. We all have our own unique gifts and skills that we bring to any endeavor. In the next chapter, I'll give you advice on how to set yourself up for success.

CHAPTER 13

Moving Past Blocks

Just like with any human endeavor, sometimes you feel like you've hit a roadblock or have plateaued. It can be frustrating to feel like something is within your grasp and you just need an extra boost to reach it. It can happen with your education, a relationship, a career, a diet, and even on your personal journey to enlightenment. I have news for you: It happens to all of us at one point or another, and I'd like to talk here about some methods that can help you get unstuck.

Knowledge Is King

Congratulations, the first step is one that you are already doing: reading! There are so many opportunities to get inspired and rejuvenated by the journeys and experiences of others. Find authors who speak to your soul. Ask for recommendations from people you trust.

Many spiritual teachers have workshops, webinars, and lectures that can assist you in moving forward on your spiritual path. You'll be surprised sometimes when you read a book on a subject that interests you, and the author will mention a topic that catches your attention. "Wow, that's fascinating!" you'll hear yourself say. Those are the subjects that your soul is drawn to. Follow its lead.

When I first met Brian Hurst in the 1980s and he told me that I, too, would be a medium, I thought he was off his rocker. But the specifics that he gave me during my very first mediumistic reading led me to believe that there was more to this New Age thing than meets the eye. I started to read anything and everything about mediumship, psychic phenomena, ghosts, and the supernatural. One book led me to another and then another. I was particularly drawn to the writings of White Eagle, Manly P. Hall, and Anthony Borgia, to name just a few. I would spend hours browsing at The Bodhi Tree on Melrose Avenue in L.A., which sadly is no longer there. I have since acquired a huge spiritual library, and I believe that the knowledge and wisdom I have gained from books are the foundation to any spiritual pursuit.

And I can't stress this enough: Not everything you read is going to resonate with you. It doesn't make it wrong; it just means that it is not for you. Embrace the pearls of wisdom that ring true to you, and manifest them into your life. Having spiritual knowledge without *living* spiritually actually seems worse to me than not having had the knowledge in the first place.

Birds of a Feather

The second step is to connect with like-minded individuals. The wonderful thing about humans is that we are all unique, but when you are working on developing your psychic, mediumistic, or healing skills, it's critical to spend time with others who share and understand your interests and goals. You are always going to have some family members or friends who think that what you're doing is "woo-woo" or "airy-fairy." I have them in my life as well. And I'm not saying that you should dump them or spend less time with them. What I am saying is: These people have their own path and you need to accept them for who they are, but you should never let them belittle you or bring you down. Accept that spirituality is not their thing. But be sure to have a support system that values your beliefs. When you form relationships with like-minded people, you are more apt to connect with Spirit and your guides; shared experiences will help you to open up to ways you had never thought about.

The Development Circle

To facilitate this meeting of the minds, consider joining or starting a development circle. A development circle consists of at least two people, and preferably no more than six people. Think of it like a book club, but instead of reviewing books, you are getting together to develop your psychic and spiritual skills more fully. Sitting in a development circle each week can facilitate your growth in becoming more adept at tuning in to

Spirit. The more we learn from others, the more we expand our knowledge. I did it as a developing medium, and I still do it to this day.

It is important that the group be harmonious and that everyone sets the same intention. If there is discord or squabbling, the negative energies can hinder the group from achieving the highest good for all. There should be a "no harm, no foul" attitude when seeking participants to create a cohesive and beneficial circle. Sometimes the energies of strangers don't gel, and that's okay; everyone will fit in somewhere.

To join an already existing development circle that is looking for new members, you can check with your local New Age bookstore or Spiritualist Church to see if they know of one that convenes in your area. If you decide to start a circle of your own, here are some guidelines.

- Meet once a week at the same time in the same place. Being a group member is a commitment, and each person must be willing to give approximately two hours of time to participate.

- As the group meets each week, spirits recognize the circle's intention and will make themselves available to come through with messages. Your guides and loved ones set aside the "time" to be with you and build up the group's energy.

- When the circle is created, one person should be picked to lead the group. This is usually someone who has a certain amount of psychic experience and spiritual awareness.

- Each circle begins with an opening prayer to welcome spirit guides, friends, and family into the circle. Ask for their assistance in protecting the group. You can say something like:

  Dear Friends,
  Come close to us and share your love and
  knowledge with us. Fill us with your inspiration
  and nurture us as we grow. Build our energy so
  that we can recognize your messages. Protect us
  from harm and always keep us safe.

- At the end of the prayer, envision a beautiful golden light surrounding the circle and the entire room for added protection.

- You may want to have some inspiring music playing in the background to help raise the energy.

- Open the circle with discussion, but keep the comments to a minimum so that you have enough time to contact Spirit. Decide on whether you want to help one particular person in the group or work together to develop every person's sensitivity. The leader should keep track of time so that everyone has a chance to participate. If one person is in need of assistance, the group can focus their mental energy on that person and surround him or her in the golden light of love. When all discussion is over, the circle members close their eyes and sit quietly.

- When spirits approach, you may feel cool breezes around your body. This is the way spirits enter the energy of the room. You may begin to see some signs in your mind like shapes in the form of circles or squares, or lights, colors, objects, faces, and random forms. This is the Spirit world. Many times the images or sensations are not familiar, and that is why you are together. You may sense something that is for someone else in the circle. You may also hear taps, knocks, or other sounds. As best as you can, remember what you are feeling, sensing, and seeing.

- You may have strange sensations in your body. These are usually spirit guides working with your aura. The energy in your aura develops more and more as you meet in the circle.

- At the conclusion of the circle, the leader informs everyone to come back to their physical awareness. Wait until everyone is safely back. The leader then says a closing prayer, thanking the spirits for helping and guiding the circle, and sending light and love to all.

Finally, everyone can share their messages, signs, and observations so that all can evaluate and review. The validation you receive from the circle will enhance the confidence you need in knowing that you have truly contacted Spirit.

Nourish Your Soul

Sometimes the obligations of everyday life can take their toll on your spiritual well-being and create a stumbling block on your path to staying high-minded. Just watching the news can put me into a funky mood. I'm blessed to have the luxury of surrounding myself with a group of people whom I enjoy and who support me; most people have bosses, co-workers, or interaction with the general public, which can sometimes bring them down. It's important to take time out of your day to process any negative energy or feelings that can impede the inspiration your guides are bestowing.

It might seem selfish to put yourself first, but when you take care of yourself, everyone in your life will benefit. The noise and activities of everyday life can drown out the voice of your soul. It's important to retreat from everyday obligations. Taking time to connect with your Divine Source each day through meditation and mindful pursuits allows your inner voice to be heard. You will have a deeper awareness and appreciation for your own spiritual gifts along with enhancing the awareness of signs from your guides and spirit loved ones.

Examine Your Intentions

If you still feel as if you haven't reached your fullest potential in having a daily relationship with your guides, it might be time to have an honest talk with yourself. Is it possible that you are creating your own roadblocks? Pause for a moment, take stock of your feelings, and examine your intentions. Fear, impatience, and denial can sabotage your progress. Have you received critical feedback or judgment from others that has caused you to back off from your quest? Is your intuition telling you something that your ego mind desperately wants to ignore? Are you tempted to give up because you're not progressing as quickly as you would like? Take time to acknowledge your feelings and write them down in your journal. Admitting your challenges and reservations is the first step toward moving past them.

Now is also a great time to assess your intentions. The primary goal in creating a foundation of values based on the counsel of your guides is to enrich your life and fulfill your soul's purpose. The byproduct of that journey is that the people around you find that their lives have been enriched as well. Your intention should always start with you, and then the ripple effect of your spiritual growth can and will benefit all those who cross your path.

CHAPTER 14

Raising Your Energy

When someone makes the transition to Spirit, it is possible for them to send signs to their loved ones who are still in a physical dimension. To communicate, however, Spirit seeks out someone who can sustain the energy needed to bridge the gap between worlds so that thought or images can be transmitted. This is true for guides as well. There is a light or luminosity around the person that makes it easy for spirits to identify them so they can project their thoughts, feelings, and visions.

To receive messages from Spirit, one needs to raise their energetic vibration as the spirits lower theirs. The pure energy of divine love is the fuel that makes this link. To sustain this link with the higher dimensions, we must be able to raise and extend our energy to have the kind of atmosphere in which Spirit can connect.

Can everyone do it? Yes! I've talked about training your mind and how to move past blocks, and now you're ready to take the next step toward developing a conscious relationship with your guides. But first, let's try a couple of experiments to gauge your current psychic abilities.

Sensing Energy

We are all born with the ability to see and feel energy. As you start to raise your energy, you'll get better and better at it. The following is an exercise I received from the Spirit world. It will help you become more aware of how sensitive you are right now so you can gauge your progress. And, it's fun to do.

Find three separate photos of people or animals you know. Make sure the photos are the same size so that your sense of touch is not a factor in distinguishing them from each other. Get a blindfold and make sure you cannot see through it. Place the photos on a table in front of you and look at each photo. Take a moment to feel connected with each photo. Now put on your blindfold and shuffle the photos. Lay them out in front of you.

Pick up each photo and feel the energy of the person/animal in the photo. Remember, it's not what you think; it's what you feel. When you sense that you have correctly identified the photos, lay them down in an order that you'll remember. Take off the blindfold and look at the photos. Did you identify them correctly?

Besides choosing the correct photo, did you sense anything as you held the photos while blindfolded? Perhaps the mood of the subject? Or the date when the photo was taken? If the photo is of a person who is still alive and available, you can always question him or her and see if you were correct in your sensing.

Reading an Energy Field

In addition to sensing energy, you also can enhance your ability to read energy. This energy can be seen around inanimate objects, but it usually remains fixed. When we speak about the energy field of a person, we call it an *aura*, and it changes constantly. Different colors of the aura represent different characteristics, but I'm not going to focus on diagnosing the aura, only your ability to see it. As you begin to practice, it probably doesn't seem that different than those Magic Eye illustrations that were so popular in the 1990s. You would focus your vision on the center of the illustration and, with practice, an image would appear.

When you practice, ask a friend to sit in front of a white background. Focus your attention between their eyebrows and let your peripheral vision detect the outline of energy surrounding them. It might look like a shadow or a light silhouette. Once you notice it, see if you can distinguish colors. The colors of the rainbow are healthy colors; browns and grays are unhealthy. Can you tell if the aura is balanced at the top, in the middle, and down at the bottom? Or do you find the top with way too much energy and barely any at the bottom? Try to sense or feel that; it is telling you the energy space is unbalanced.

The next step is to sense whether one side feels stronger than the other. Do you see blotches or denseness more on one side than the other? I call these blotches *energy pockets*. Can you tell if these energy pockets feel hotter or cooler in temperature, and if so, on which side? Focus on the pockets of energy. I want you to learn how to interpret them. Do they contain emotional, physical, mental, or spiritual energy? If the pocket of energy is around the heart, does it have to do with an emotional upset, like grief or sadness? Or is the pocket mostly around the top of the head? It may be spiritual in nature. For instance, maybe the person has given up on his or her connection to the Source? Does the person feel undeserving? Are the blotches brown and dark? Maybe the person is mentally drained. Try to interpret what kind of block is in the energy field.

Next, sense the colors around parts of the body. I call this the *rainbow connection*. Every single person has colors—like the colors of a rainbow—red, yellow, orange, green, blue, indigo, and violet. Sense which part has more red or more orange. Is there yellow around the head area? Yellow is mental energy. Is there a particular part that looks green? Even though green is the color of the heart chakra, you may sense green around a foot because a person may have a swollen ankle, and green is working to heal that area.

Give yourself permission to sense and be open. Again, set your intention: *I am going to sense the energy, color, and value of this person or place.* Remember, you may feel energy very differently than someone else, so don't compare. Being aware of the energy field may not happen right away. Practice, practice, practice. Reading the aura is like learning a different language.

To raise your energy, you will use the breath and run energy through the chakra points. Your chakras need to be functioning at an optimal level in order for your energy to build. When you make an effort every day to focus on your chakra points and make sure that they are healthy and unblocked, your energetic body is vibrating sufficiently for the messages of your spirit guides to enter your conscious mind.

Chakra Points

The human body contains hundreds of locations where there is focused and concentrated energy. But there are seven main chakra points that you need to be aware of in order to raise your energy.

Chakra is a Sanskrit word meaning "wheel." The seven common chakras spin like wheels or vortexes of light and color in the etheric body. These chakras receive, transmit, and process physical, mental, emotional, and spiritual energies and interconnect like lines on a grid to create a magnetic field of energy. It's important to acknowledge each chakra to see that its health and vibrancy are ideal. Each of the seven main chakras is a microcosm of color, tonality, and density forming a network of energy that interacts and overlaps into one holistic system. Before I lead you on a chakra meditation, let me introduce them to you.

- 1st or Root Chakra. Located at the base of the spine, this is our connection to Mother Earth through our feet, legs, spinal column, bones, and lower body. The color is red and represents vitality and life force. Lessons associated with this chakra are security, courage, mastery of body, grounding, balance, and patience.

- 2nd or Sacral Chakra. Located two inches below the belly button, this is our connection to water through our reproductive glands, spleen, and bladder. The color is orange and represents sexuality, intimacy, and nourishment. This is the first of our three emotional centers. Lessons associated with this chakra are giving and receiving, raw desires, addictions, passion, and tolerance.

- 3rd or Solar Plexus Chakra. Located in the middle of the tummy, this is our connection to fire. The color is yellow and represents our digestive system, metabolism, emotions, pancreas, sympathetic nervous system, and muscles. This is the second of our emotional centers. It acts like a radio transmitter. It is the seat of knowingness, as in *go with your gut* or *gut feelings*. Lessons associated with this chakra are ego, willpower, self-control, fear, humor, and immortality. The silver cord that connects the physical body with the spiritual body is in this chakra. When we die this cord is disconnected, and we move into the spiritual dimensions.

- 4th or Heart Chakra. Located in the center of the chest, this is my favorite chakra. It is our connection to air and our sense of touch. The color is green; the secondary color is pink. This chakra represents our heart, blood, circulation, thymus, arms, legs, skin, and lungs. This is the third emotional center that anchors the higher spiritual self with the lower physical self. The three emotional chakras are used for clairsentience or clear-feeling. Lessons associated with this chakra include divine and unconditional love, empathy, forgiveness, compassion, depression, emotional instability, group consciousness, balance, and contentment.

- 5th or Throat Chakra. Located in the neck, this is the center for clairaudience and our sense of hearing. This is our connection to the ethereal dimension. The color is sky blue and represents speech, creativity, communication, thyroid, voice, esophagus, and larynx. Lessons associated with this chakra include expression, the arts, inspiration, honesty, gentleness, and speaking up for ourselves. It acts like a bridge between our thoughts and feelings.

- 6th or Brow Chakra. Known as the "third eye," this chakra is located in the center of the forehead. It is the center for clairvoyance or clear-seeing. This is our connection to electricity and the seat of consciousness. The color is indigo or dark blue and represents the pituitary gland, face, ears, cerebellum, central nervous system, and left eye. We receive with our left eye. This is the center of psychic awareness and mind-to-mind communication. Lessons associated with this chakra are intuition, imagination, wisdom, devotion, cynicism, vision problems, perception, and higher mindedness.

- 7th or Crown Chakra. Located at the top of the head, this is our connection to light and pure being. The color is violet and represents the pineal gland, cerebral cortex, thought, and right eye. We give out through our right eye. We download higher truths and the divine aspects through this chakra. It is the doorway to the infinite. Lessons associated with this chakra are selfless service, perception beyond our senses, confusion, and separation from and connection to the One Source.

When our chakras are spinning in a clockwise direction, they are healthy and powerful. Raising our energy through our chakra points is the best way to create an inner environment that will give us the ability to contact Spirit and our guides.

Grounding Your Energy

It is important that when you work with your various chakras and build your power, you are properly grounded. This is the first step to allowing Spirit to blend with your energy so that you can receive messages from your guides. As with all meditations, establish yourself in a comfortable space where you won't be disturbed. You may choose to be in a dim room and/or to play tranquil music in the background.

Grounding Meditation

Sit in a comfortable chair with your back straight. Close your eyes and let your thoughts pass through your mind. Focus on your body: Starting with your feet on the floor, move up to your legs, back, stomach, chest, shoulders, neck, and head. Get a sense of what your body feels like. Take a deep breath for a count of seven and exhale for a count of seven. With each breath, become more aware of your human body, heart, cells, tissues, and so forth. Observe the body without judgment. Continue to slowly inhale and exhale for a count of seven a few more times.

Your breath brings you to a different level of awareness. Focus your awareness on your heart chakra in the center of your chest. As you concentrate on your heart space, be mindful that you are a soul having a human experience, and the truth of your being is way beyond the boundaries of your body. Let the green light of this chakra spin and fill your consciousness with feelings of love and peace.

As your heart chakra continues to spin, slowly move your awareness down to your root chakra. It is at the base of your spine and spinning red light. Visualize the energy in your root chakra moving through the bottom of your feet and going down to connect to the center of Mother Earth. Inhale for the count of seven, and exhale slowly, feeling connected to the solid, secure, balanced Earth energy. Imagine that you are like a tree with roots going straight to the core of Mother Earth.

As Mother Earth holds you in her embrace, realize that as a soul you have a beautiful connection with the Spirit world and your Higher Self. The true divine aspect of your being exists on a cosmic level. You are connected to these higher realms through a beam of light that starts at the top of your head and travels up to a distant, beautiful golden star. This soul energy emanates from the spinning violet light of your crown chakra. As you inhale, your awareness rises higher and higher, getting closer to the star. Exhale, and be there in that beautiful golden light. As you breathe, you become aware of this energy—the lightness and subtleness of it. This beautiful cosmic, golden, spiritual light surrounds you.

Become aware of the subtle difference between the Earth and cosmic energies. You are part of all these energies.

As you inhale, bring the golden light through the crown chakra, into the third eye, then down into the throat to your heart space, while at same time, bring the grounding energy up through your feet, solar plexus, and into the heart space. Both energies meet and meld together into a fountain of energy. Run the energy up and down and out through your heart chakra. Inhale, bringing down the cosmic energy and bringing up the Earth energy; exhale, sending it forth in front of you through your heart.

Continue to run your energy as you inhale and exhale over and over again at your own pace. Do it slowly, running the energy slowly as you inhale and exhale. Let this blending of the two energies become familiar to you. Let your heart be a neutral space as you run your energy. As you become familiar with these energies, you will expand your perception all around you. You'll be aware of energies and spirit beings as they enter your space. You are able to telepathically converse with these beings and guides.

> *When you feel your energy start to wane, slowly become aware of your feet on the ground. Let the cosmic light come back down through your crown chakra. Bless Mother Earth for her protection as you bring your energy back up into your spinning root chakra. When you are comfortable and totally aware of your body in this space, slowly open your eyes.*

Increase Your Heart Space

To create an inviting energy for your guides and to improve the conditions for them to communicate with you, it is important to maintain a healthy heart space. This is one of the exercises I teach in my workshops to help students use their heart chakra to expand their love.

Heart Space

Close your eyes and take in some deep breaths. Inhale and exhale while focusing on the spinning green energy of your heart chakra. With every exhalation, imagine the green light growing like a balloon. This balloon represents your loving heart energy. It begins to fill the room, and then goes beyond the room. Your energy of love is a beacon for your guides. They understand your intent—that you have created this place in the physical dimension for them to visit. They feel safe and at home in the love energy that you have provided.

As you sit in this space, breathe in joy and exhale all the stored-up stress, negative thinking, limitations, and judgments you have been holding onto, whether about yourself or someone else. Give them all over to your Higher Self to release and clear out. You are surrounded by loving beings who thank you for creating this space. They know that they are always welcome. When you are ready, slowly open your eyes. Become aware of your body and surroundings. One more deep breath in and out. You can now come back to your body feeling refreshed and alert.

Whenever you have feelings of indecision or confusion, you now have the tools to create a space for the wisdom of the guides to advise you. With practice, you can do this exercise anywhere or anytime you feel the need. It can take just seconds for you to create your heart space and invite your guides in.

Raising Your Energy

The Earth dimension is a heavy and not particularly comfortable place for Spirit. It is up to you to make the effort to meet spirit guides halfway. Now that you've learned to ground yourself and how to expand your heart space, you are ready to raise your energy. When I raise my energy, I picture a geyser of energy pouring from my chakras and surrounding me. The combined colors create a blinding white energy field that envelops me. I know that I am in the center of my power. I invite spirit guides to come into this space.

Practice raising your power. Acknowledge your own power. You need to sustain that power. Remember, spirits have to slow down their energy to your level, and you have to raise yours to theirs. If you feel your energy drop into the solar plexus area, you are in the psychic area. You want to raise your power back up to above your head to the spiritual area. Become familiar with your power. Raising your power will sustain your energy levels in whatever you do.

White Light

Make yourself comfortable in a position where you feel that your chakras are in perfect alignment from the top of your head to the base of your spine. Close your eyes and take several deep breaths in and out. Focus once again on the divinity in your heart center. Visualize the spinning green energy of your heart chakra. Take your time and enjoy the feeling of your burgeoning heart space. As you breathe in, become aware of your divinity, your perfection, and your own spiritual self. As you breathe out, release any thoughts, fears, anxieties, and unwanted emotional turmoil.

Sense an energy percolating and bubbling up from your toes, through your legs, and then to the base of your spine. This energy ignites the spinning red of your root chakra. Your physical body must know that it is safe and anchored before you can allow the energy to continue up to the sacral chakra. Feel the spinning orange energy in the pit of your stomach—it makes you feel alive and fills your being with a passion for truth. As the energy builds, it reaches your solar plexus. This is the seat of your intuition and the whirling yellow sphere of this chakra lets you know that all is well and safe.

The energy continues up your spine, through the green wheel of your already spinning heart chakra, to your throat chakra. The blue pinwheel of this spinning chakra lets your guides know your intention is to communicate with them. The energy passes through your third eye and sets the indigo wheel of energy into motion. As it spins, endorphins are released into your bloodstream, making you feel centered in knowingness and love.

As the energy reaches the top of your head, it activates the indigo of the crown chakra. The energy that now carries the color of every chakra emanates from the top of your head as a bright white light. This is your light, and it surrounds you. Fill the atmosphere around you with the energy of enthusiasm, joy, and love. This is your energy—your own enthusiasm.

CHAPTER 15

MAKING CONTACT

There are several ways to meet your guides; you'll find what works best for you with practice. As a medium, the first thing I do before a reading or a demonstration in front of an audience is to establish my team of guides. I will sit and meditate, open my energy centers, and run my energy. By doing this I create a sacred space around me. It shows the Spirit world that I am ready to work and that they can step into my space and influence my thought.

The next thing I do is ask my guide, the gatekeeper, to come close to me. When my guide is in place, I know the door is open to the Spirit world. Several guides usually come around and stand behind me, above my head, and on my shoulders. The fascinating thing is that every time I do an event, I may have two or three guides who are familiar, and several guides I don't recognize. I can tell they are guides because of the energy—it is a quickening energy—a higher form of love and joy that is different from a regular spirit. I realize that the unknown guides are there either to help the audience to be more receptive or they are guides of the audience members for whom I am reading. When all guides are in place, I establish the link and open the portal for spirits to enter. My gatekeeper ushers them in one at a time.

In order to contact your guides, you, too, must establish a sacred space where they can work with you. In the previous chapters, I explained the energy centers and how to run your energy. In this chapter I will present exercises for contacting your guide.

As I mentioned, guides can come in and out of our sphere of influence depending on what is going on in our lives. We make agreements with some guides before our incarnation to stay with us the whole time. Our guides are eager to help because it's a learning opportunity for them as well; they evolve spiritually as you do.

There may be a karmic obligation for your guide to assist you in this life. Or, your guides may be with you in this life because they did not live up to their optimal potential in a former life, and helping you is a way to express their capabilities. Or they could have done a better job at learning the golden rule while on Earth and, by being of service to you, they fulfill a responsibility previously ignored. Many times, guides are family members who couldn't express themselves on Earth, but in the Spirit world, they have more freedom to be who they truly are, and serve us best from the other side. Always, spirit family members want to create happier conditions for their loved ones on Earth.

Before you begin each exercise, start with your grounding and breathing techniques, opening your chakras, and running your energy up and down your body and out through your heart center. Remember to keep your journal with you and write down any words or insights that your guide gives to you.

Getting to Know Your Guide

The title of the section is actually a bit of a misnomer since you already know your guide. And you know each other very well. You've met and had conversations an infinite number of times before—but it was subconsciously. Here, I'm talking about *consciously* meeting and knowing your guide.

The following meditation was passed on to me from my friend Mavis Pittilla. She once recounted this story to me about how she began her spiritual journey and eventually met her guide.

"I was quite cross at God at the time," she told me. "I had an illness, and I wondered, *Why is this happening to me?* I was in my lounge at home when suddenly a spirit stood in front of me—an ordinary working-class man. He wasn't a ghost or an apparition, but someone as solid as you. He said, *Go find a healer or you won't hear the New Year bells.*

"I didn't know what to make of the encounter, and when I told my husband about it, he was naturally concerned for my mental health. But what puzzled me was that I was already under a doctor's care at the time. *I already have a healer*, I thought. *What did the spirit man mean about a healer?*

"Through a series of 'coincidences' (but I call it destiny), my husband met a chap at work and told him about my visitation. 'I think my wife is having a breakdown,' my husband confided as he finished the story. The man replied, 'I think I know what she's talking about. I'm a spiritual healer.' While I continued my conventional medical care, I went to this man for the laying on of hands for months, and here I am today. That man who appeared in the lounge of my home not only saved my life, he opened a gateway to explore my mediumistic path.

WISDOM FROM YOUR SPIRIT GUIDES

"While this spirit man in my lounge did spark my spiritual journey, it was later that I met my main guide, Mikosan, and in one of my many conversations with him, he encouraged me to commune with other guides and inspirers by using a technique that I call 'a room with a view.'"

Just a quick word about expectations before you do Mavis's meditation: Don't have any preconceived notions about what your guide will look like. They may present themselves as how *they* feel the most comfortable or as how *you* will feel the most comfortable. I am not going to use *he* or *she* when referencing your guide. They may present themselves as non-gender specific, or even nonhuman. Communication between the two of you may be nonverbal, or you may speak just like old friends having a cup of tea. Your guide knows what is best for this meeting, so just follow their lead. I have tweaked the meditation that Mikosan shared with Mavis to fit my own preference; you must feel free to do the same.

The Meeting Room

Close your eyes, and once again become mindful of your space. Be aware of the space below, above, to your right, and to your left. Begin your breathing technique. As you inhale, let the energy come up from the earth into your feet and move up into your body. Take another breath, and let the energy from the cosmos—the golden light—come through the top of your head. These energies meet in your heart space. Run your energy up and down and out through your heart chakra. Continue to breathe and become aware of your heart space as the seat of your soul. Feel comfortable and relaxed in this state before you continue.

Use your imagination and visualize a beautiful room that is square in shape. One whole wall of the room is taken up by a huge window that looks out into a garden. Some of the window panes are open to let in a soft, perfumed breeze. Begin to fill the room with everything you love. It could be furniture, paintings, sculpture, photographs, flowers, lighting, books, and so forth. Fill the room with everything that represents you. It could be a lot of items or only a few; it doesn't matter. But in the center of the room, you'll want to place two chairs facing each other. Fill the four corners of the room with your loving energy. This room feels like you—it is your soul's room—and it is the place where you will meet your guide.

Sit in the chair facing the window. Look out into the beautiful sunny garden. There are rolling hills of green, and your favorite trees and flowers are dotted among them. As you are relaxed looking out the window, you notice that the light is becoming brighter outside. The whole window is filled with a beautiful white light. Your spirit guide has arrived to meet you in your soul room. You can say:

Dear spirit guide, you are most welcome to join me.

The being comes through the window and fills the room with more love than you have ever felt; indeed, this being knows everything about you, loves you unconditionally, and always has your best interests at heart. Let the guide express itself as it comes in and sits in front of you in the chair.

With a clear and open mind, your guide impresses onto you the answers to your first questions. These could be:

- What name shall I call you?

- Have you ever incarnated on Earth?

> - *Why have we agreed for you to be my guide?*
>
> - *Do you have a particular mission to help me with?*
>
> - *What information do you have for me right now?*
>
> *Listen in your heart to what your guide has to say. Remember, you have many more meetings like this planned, so don't overdo it the first time. When the time has come, your meeting ends, and your guide leaves through the open window.*
>
> *Once again, bring your awareness back to this physical dimension. Take some deep breaths and become of your body sitting in your chair. Feel your feet planted on the ground and let your energy dissipate up through the top of your head. Slowly open your eyes.*

Write in your journal anything that your guide shared with you. The more you do this exercise and the more you personalize it, the more expansive it will become. Other guides and inspirers will be attracted to this room that you have created for them.

Receive, Organize, Apply

When I write a book, I go through three stages. The first is downloading the information and thoughts onto paper. The second is organizing the information. The third is making sure that it makes sense for the reader. The analogy I use is building a car engine. The first stage is to lay all the parts out on the ground. The second is to put the parts in the car. The third is to make sure that the car runs. I think the same is true for the information that you receive from your guide during meditation. You need all three stages for the contact to be successful and meaningful, but everyone is going to have their favorite/more-manageable stage of the process.

I personally am much more of a *downloading the information* person. I really enjoy receiving information from my guide. The process of organizing what information fits into which aspect of my life, and then determining how to actually apply it in my life, doesn't come as easily. I've gotten better at it with practice, but it's just the way my human brain is hardwired. I love the jolt of inspiration; it's the follow-through that I have had trouble with. I have to keep reminding myself that the first stage without the second and third is meaningless.

The reason I mention this is because after doing your meditation with your guide, you, too, might have trouble with a part of the process. What I can tell you is that it gets easier with time and practice. Always be sure to have your journal with you after all meditations. Some things will come through from your guides that don't make sense at the time, but if you have them written down for future reference, you won't have to worry about forgetting anything.

As I've mentioned before, having spiritual knowledge without applying it—or living it—in your everyday interactions is wasteful. The wisdom that you receive from your guide is not meant for others to live by; it's meant for you. It's the whole reason why you have decided to have a conscious relationship with your guide.

Mind Meld

As you develop a stronger conscious connection with your guide, you'll find that the meditation in your soul room is not always necessary. I would advise using it when you want to meet a new guide, but once you have met your guide several times in the soul room, you'll find that making contact can be as easy as thinking about it.

When I want to communicate with one of my guides, I simply take a few deep breaths and become mindful of the space around me (as in no negativity). I send out a thought to my guide, calling it by name. Spirit people live in a mental world—thoughts are as real to them as words are to us. Those in Spirit can see, feel, and hear thought. They always know when we are thinking of them. This exercise will help you to blend your thoughts and energy with that of your spirit guide. As you get better at this, make an agreement with your guide on a signal so that you know you have made conscious contact. It could be a physical sensation, a feeling, or a telepathic symbol.

The Invitation

Relax and clear your mind. Take a few deep breaths, create a space in your mind, and invite your guide to come close. You can telepathically say:

Welcome, _____, please come to mind. Let me know that you are here with me.

You will get a sign that your guide is present. Don't force it; put aside your ego and surrender to the impressions, feelings, and visions you are about to receive. You have to be as open-minded as you can. Immediately you will feel the space changing. It will feel illuminated. Invite your guide into your space. Merge your energies into one. When you are ready, you can say:

I am in need of your assistance. Share any information that you have for me.

As you sit with your guide in your space, you may sense some thoughts being projected into your mind. Let the guide download into your mind any feelings, thoughts, or symbols. Sit with your guide and listen to his or her teaching and philosophy. When it is time to stop, you can say:

Dear _____ , I bless you and thank you for joining me and sharing your advice.

Take some deep breaths and slowly come back into your body. Become aware of your feet, then your legs, and upward to your head. Inhale and exhale a few more times. Raise your arms and center yourself.
Slowly open your eyes.

This is a great technique to use if you are not at home and not near the room you use for your meditations. You can do this anywhere as long as you have created a loving space. And don't do it while you're driving!

Greeting Your Etheric Council

After 30 years of spiritual work, I have come to believe in the existence of highly evolved beings who work in tandem with spirit guides and assist the brave souls who have agreed to incarnate. They may be called *masters, the elders,* or *the wise ones,* but I like the term *etheric council.* Your etheric council is always aware of your day-to-day life, but they are most involved in your pre-birth incarnation decisions, major life changes (marriages, births of children, deaths of loved ones), and, of course, the death of your own earthly body.

Don't think of the council as a panel of judges, for it is not their role to criticize or condemn. Far from it. The council is made up of beings specific to you, and their only role is one of guidance, support, and love. The wisdom of the council is filtered to you through your spirit guide, but it *is* possible to greet your etheric council. The encounter can be immensely profound.

The Etheric Council

Close your eyes. Begin your breathing and grounding exercise and run your energy. As you run energy and expand your heart space to get into a receptive mode, send a thought to the Spirit world:

Dear spirit friends, I am going on a journey to greet my council. I want to acknowledge my love for them and be aware of any teaching that they want to bestow upon me.

As you sit in your sacred space, envision a shaft of light emanating from the top of your head. There is upward movement in the shaft as it stretches beyond your vision.

Put your conscious awareness inside the shaft and let it take you up, up, and away from your physical body. Your breathing is even, and you are at peace as your awareness travels farther upward. As you go higher and higher, you become aware that you are traveling beyond space and time, past planets, solar systems, and a myriad of colors and lights.

Your motion starts to slow and the shaft of light opens. Before you is a beautiful marble building. This is the hall of learning in the etheric world. The beautiful building, inlaid with gems and pearls, beckons to you. Your awareness floats toward it, feeling the familiarity as if you've been here many times before. You enter the hall of learning and all around are bookcases as far and as tall as you can see. The books are leather-bound, of various colors, and glow in the dim light. This is the celestial library. One book in particular glows brighter than the others. You approach it and see that your name is embossed on the cover. You slide it off the shelf and hold it close. This is the book of your soul. This book belongs to you but it is kept here for you.

The opening of a huge mahogany door catches your attention. A bright light filters through the opening as you float toward it, still holding your book. You enter a beautiful room that is glistening with white light. You look up and see round windows in the ceiling. There are seven windows, each one a different color: violet, indigo, blue, green, yellow, orange, and red. The rays of colored light shine down through the windows, but when they meet they bathe a long table in pure white light.

Seated at the table is your etheric council. The love that you feel from them is indescribable. You feel waves of appreciation from them that you have made the effort to meet them with your conscious awareness. As you sit at the table with them, you acknowledge each one, and the sense that you have known them throughout eternity is overwhelming. Telepathically, you pick up a thought that is really made of several thoughts of your council. They have melded their thoughts into one. They are telling you about the book that you're holding. They invite you to open it. The pages are filled with beautiful cursive handwriting. The book is all about your soul, and the council lets you know that you are always free to come to the library and read it. The book is here to help you.

There are many blank pages in the book of your soul. You look up at the council questioningly. The message you receive is that this is the part of your current life that has yet to be written. The council asks your permission to let them help you write it. In fact, they are enthusiastic and optimistic about what a beautiful story you can all write together.

The council invites you to visit anytime. You express your gratitude for their involvement in your life and for reminding you that you are a wonderful vessel of light for all those on Earth. They are so proud of you for agreeing to incarnate into the physical for the betterment of all. The council blesses you and reminds you that they will always be here for you.

You float back through the open mahogany door and return your soul book to its place on the shelf. As you descend the steps of the hall, you see your shaft of light in the garden beckoning you. You enter it and descend down through space until you see your body still relaxing comfortably. The shaft of light places your awareness back into your body.

Take a few deep breaths and focus on your feet, bringing the energy up through your body and out the top of your head until you are fully back in your body. Feel the happiness and joy in your body. Open your eyes and know that you are fully inspired.

You'll want to take a moment to process your visit to the council. Review it quietly in your head. When you're ready, get your journal and write down everything you remember. You'll also want to write down questions for your next visit. You are welcome to return as often as you'd like; this realm is not foreign to you. It is your true home.

The power to contact your guide and to visit your etheric council has always been with you. It is your birthright as a soul, but reincarnation doesn't come with a user's guide. These tools have to be sought out on your own, and it is your guides who lead you to this information. I hope this book has been helpful on your journey to discover the power inside of you. I thank you for spending this time with me, and I thank your guides for leading you here.

EPILOGUE

During the months that I was working on this book, I did something I thought I would never do: I took a hot-air balloon ride! In the new town that I live in, balloons are constantly overhead. In fact, there is an empty lot across from the market where I shop, and the balloons actually fill up and launch from there. It is quite an overwhelming sight. The possibility of actually taking a ride intrigued me, but I don't even like to fly in planes, so I pushed the thought away.

My brother-in-law Mike was coming down to visit us for his birthday. Brian thought it would be a great idea to celebrate by doing a balloon ride, so I signed on. As we prepared to board, the first thing the pilot said was: "I have no idea how long we will be up here. The moment we get up we will be looking for a place to land. We have to surrender completely to the direction of the wind." His words struck me as a good analogy for our life here on Earth—we don't know how long we will be here, but we must go wherever the wind takes us—or *wherever we are guided.*

As our rainbow balloon rose into the sky, I was struck by the quiet and peacefulness. I was expecting it to be windy, but the captain said, "If we were stationary, it would be. But we're moving *with* the wind." To the east of us were rolling green hills dotted with houses, and to the west was the Pacific Ocean. With all the traveling I do, I was surprised that my perspective in a hot-air balloon was so different from in an airplane. Maybe it's because we were drifting along on air currents without windows or pressurized cabins separating us from the sky.

On the drive back home, as we were reminiscing about the trip, the analogies between reincarnation and the balloon ride started to pour in: I had agreed to leave the comfort of my home, where I am perfectly content with my feet on the ground, to partake in an adventure that frightened and excited me. I climbed into the basket—which is like a birth—and I was in another world for an unknown amount of time. While I was up there, I put my faith in the expertise of the captain. The ride, which I had expected to be turbulent, was surprisingly calm, due to the fact that the balloon surrendered to the changing currents. And what had seemed scary turned out to be very pleasant.

When we landed and crawled out of the basket, we were back "home," and we celebrated our trip, talking about how much we had learned and how proud of ourselves we were that we had actually done it. The captain, uncorking the champagne, said, "Thank you for joining us on this adventure. It was a pleasure being your sky guide."

Remember, I was actually in the process of writing this book when we took the balloon ride. Could my guides have sent me a better message to let me know that I was on the right track?

Acknowledgments

I want to thank all my guides who are assisting me from the Spirit realms, and also the people in my life who have given me guidance and support here on Earth: Brian Preston, the Fortune family, the Barry family, the Opitz family, the Preston family, Mary Ann Saxon, Kelly Dennis, Joerdie Fisher, Joe Skeehan, Jacquie Ochoa-Rosellini, Scott Schwimer, Ron Oyer, Ken Robb, Christian Dickens, Cyndi Schacher, Peggy Fitzsimmons, Kellee White, Tori Mitchell, Mavis Pittilla, Jean Else, Lynn Probert, Tony Stockwell, Marilyn Whall, Jeff Eisenberg, Liz Cooke, Melissa Searing, Chip McAllister, Roberta Kent, Linda Tomchin, Emily Manning, and everyone at Hay House.

ABOUT THE AUTHOR

Internationally renowned #1 *New York Times* bestselling author of *Talking to Heaven, Reaching to Heaven, Healing Grief, Heaven and Earth, Looking Beyond, Meditations, Ghosts Among Us, Unfinished Business, Growing Up in Heaven, Adventures of the Soul*, and *How to Heal a Grieving Heart* (co-authored with Doreen Virtue), James Van Praagh is hailed throughout the world as a pioneer of the mediumship movement and recognized as one of the most accurate spiritual mediums working today. His messages have brought solace, peace, and spiritual insights, changing millions' view of both life and death. He has received many awards for his dedication to raising the consciousness of the planet.

James has appeared on virtually every national radio and television show, including *Oprah, Larry King Live, Dr. Phil, 48 Hours, The View, The Joy Behar Show, Chelsea Lately, Coast to Coast*, and many more. He was the host of his own nationally syndicated show, *Beyond*, which is still seen in markets around the world. James has also been a successful producer for CBS, creating *Living with the Dead*, a miniseries based on his life starring Ted Danson, and *The Dead Will Tell*, starring Eva Longoria. He was the creator and executive producer of CBS's long-running series *Ghost Whisperer*, starring Jennifer Love Hewitt.

James recently launched the James Van Praagh School of Mystical Arts, a labor of love that was years in the making. The online school offers a variety of learning experiences, from professional certifications to audio and video courses, with live calls and online forums. For more information about the James Van Praagh School of Mystical Arts, go to www.jvpschoolofmysticalarts.com.

Fans of James can tune in to his popular Hay House Radio show, *Talking to Spirit*, every Tuesday at 11 A.M. Pacific, and enjoy his online television series, *Spirit Talk*, on Gaia.com. He also shares insights and messages from the Spirit realm through his website and blog at www.vanpraagh.com and via social media.

Hay House Titles of Related Interest

YOU CAN HEAL YOUR LIFE, the movie,
starring Louise Hay & Friends
(available as an online streaming video)
www.hayhouse.com/louise-movie

THE SHIFT, the movie,
starring Dr. Wayne W. Dyer
(available as an online streaming video)
www.hayhouse.com/the-shift-movie

❀   ❀   ❀

*MEDICAL MEDIUM: Secrets Behind Chronic and Mystery Illness
and How to Finally Heal,* by Anthony William

THE TOP TEN THINGS DEAD PEOPLE WANT TO TELL YOU,
by Mike Dooley

TUNE IN: Let Your Intuition Guide You to Fulfillment and Flow,
by Sonia Choquette

*UNCHARTED: The Journey through Uncertainty
to Infinite Possibility,* by Colette Baron-Reid

All of the above are available at your local bookstore,
or may be ordered by contacting Hay House (see next page).

❀   ❀   ❀

Hay House Podcasts
Bring Fresh, Free Inspiration Each Week!

Hay House proudly offers a selection of life-changing audio content via our most popular podcasts!

Hay House Meditations Podcast

Features your favorite Hay House authors guiding you through meditations designed to help you relax and rejuvenate. Take their words into your soul and cruise through the week!

Dr. Wayne W. Dyer Podcast

Discover the timeless wisdom of Dr. Wayne W. Dyer, world-renowned spiritual teacher and affectionately known as "the father of motivation." Each week brings some of the best selections from the 10-year span of Dr. Dyer's talk show on Hay House Radio.

Hay House Podcast

Enjoy a selection of insightful and inspiring lectures from Hay House Live events, listen to some of the best moments from previous Hay House Radio episodes, and tune in for exclusive interviews and behind-the-scenes audio segments featuring leading experts in the fields of alternative health, self-development, intuitive medicine, success, and more! Get motivated to live your best life possible by subscribing to the free Hay House Podcast.

Find Hay House podcasts on iTunes, or visit www.HayHouse.com/podcasts for more info.